to Jessica

And There's More

Best wishes

Mmrs Nurds

x

And There's More

MY AUTOBIOGRAPHY
Volume Two

Chris Needs

For Gabe and Sam

First impression: 2009

The publishers wish to acknowledge the support of
Cyngor Llyfrau Cymru

Editor: Gabe Cameron
Cover photograph: Darryl Corner

ISBN: 9781847711489

Published, printed and bound in Wales by
Y Lolfa Cyf., Talybont, Ceredigion SY24 5HE
website www.ylolfa.com
e-mail ylolfa@ylolfa.com
tel 01970 832 304
fax 01970 832 782

CHAPTER ONE

On Reflection

Here I go again

FIRSTLY, MAY I SAY a big thank you if you have read my first book *Like It Is*. While I was writing it, I was panicking in case I didn't have enough material to finish it. When the book came out I realised that there was so much more that I didn't include; enough stuff in my mind to write at least another two books! So here I go again.

My life at the moment? Turmoil. Absolute turmoil. I seem to have no pleasure in life, only work. I feel as if I use my partner Gabe as a minder or a solicitor, and I really do feel that we should be having a better life together. I love what I do in the radio studio, i.e. talking to people and, of course, the music. But is it worth it?

There are still so many things that you don't know about, such as the threats on my life, and the poison pen letters, all from people wanting me dead or out of the equation. I still get a lot of insults about my sexuality and this makes it much harder to hang on to the job. It's really hard being 'known', being in the public eye constantly *and* being gay. It seems that if you are a rugby player or some top sportsperson, you won't be bothered. You're just one of the lads. But for me, this situation has become too hard to bear. (But trust me, I'm not going anywhere!)

I'm even questioned about whether I should have a

godson. Some people here in Wales have been really cruel to me. Once when Gabe and I were standing outside the shops in Cwmafan, a woman shouted across the road, 'Which one of you two's the woman?' So I shouted back across the road, 'Me. I've had it all taken away!' I still feel an air of disapproval when I go back to Cwmafan.

Since reading in the first book that I was abused when I was younger, some people have asked me, 'Who messed with you, then?' Just so they could spread the dreaded news. It's so bloody typical. And nasty emails? I get my fair share. One lady in particular constantly annoys me, and I guess it could be thought of as frightening as she sends me an itinerary of my movements; dates, times and everything. I just wish she would wake up and realise that for obvious reasons she can not have me!

I just get on with it now and hope that the idiots leave me alone and let me get on with my life. I'm beginning to downsize things at the moment, so that if I have to move or change my lifestyle, I can do so at the drop of a hat. I'm desperately trying to get Gabe to live abroad in the sun. Benidorm would be nice. There would be work there for me and I could sing, DJ and call bingo in front of happy holiday makers once again. No expensive petrol, no income tax, no 'chavs' and no moaning old gits calling me a queer... and, oh, no rain!

I thought my autobiography would have given me some closure on certain delicate matters but I feel as if it's made them worse. When the newspapers started reporting the sexual abuse, I felt as if everyone was looking at me as if I had two heads and were saying, 'Awww, there, there!'

Worst of all I was constantly asked who it was that had abused me – nosey or what? Bloody typical. So I give them all the same answer: 'Trust me. You don't really want to know... if you know what I mean.'

However, I was comforted at the BBC by Adrian Masters

from the news department who really was a great help. As was Derek Brockway. Everywhere I went people were frightened to say 'How are you?' in case I got upset or maybe told them off.

I've received some letters from religious bigots about a comment I made in my last book that I wished my abuser would 'rot in hell'. I was sternly told that I wasn't a Christian and that I had to forgive this man. My answer was that Jesus could forgive but I'm not Jesus. I'm Chris Needs and I don't profess to be as perfect as the Lord. I try to be a good follower of Him, but I don't think for one minute that I'll match Him at all.

I seem to get hurt and used; most of all by family, but occasionally by friends too. I know I'm too giving and trusting, and I always come out the loser, but it has always been part of my nature. My mother always said, 'The more you give, the less you are thought of.' I have always tried to give anyone and everyone a helping hand if they were short of work, say, or money. But often I find that I have been shat on from the greatest heights. I am slowly turning into a hard little bugger and I don't really want to, but these users have made me this way.

What if I met the teacher who used to call me names and hit me about the head when I was at school? I'd like to see what he has to say for himself. To be honest, I couldn't be bothered to make enquiries to see if he's still 'with us'. There are other times when I feel so much hatred that I wouldn't know where to begin. But what would I gain?

So here I am once again writing away for a release... and hoping my VAT bill isn't too much this time. Ah, life is good!

CHAPTER TWO

Village Life and My Mother

Like a pensioner's leg

MY MOTHER, MARGARET ROSE, was worse than me in the mornings, and if I was ever late for school she would push me through the door with a piece of bread and butter in my gob, wiping my face with some spit on a hanky.

When she had the shop I'd make sure that she had her lunch on the table or, should I say, on her lap. She was always on a diet – chicken with the skin taken off, salad, Nimble bread with low-fat spread, and then apple tart and thick custard for afters.

My father Harold (or 'Aitch' as everyone called him) took breakfast in bed to my mother every morning. Her favourite was laverbread on toast, with tea and a tea towel because she always spilled it everywhere.

After doing the clubs at night I would return home with a cartload of curry – all different sorts – and my mother would come downstairs, eat three-quarters of it and deny it the following day. She'd say, *'Ti'n siarad trw dy dwll,'* which basically meant, 'You're talking through your arse.' My God, she loved her food. She really did live to eat. She'd eat a whole trifle on her own and anything else left over! She'd always say that there were lots of starving children in Africa and we should never waste.

With my mother it would quite often turn out that I

became the parent and she became the child. If ever I said to her, 'Now come along, Mother, it's time to be getting back to the house,' she'd simply reply, 'Oh, chill out for **** sake.'

Well, one day I remember I took my mother out shopping in Cardiff Bay. When we came out of the supermarket she kept staring at something in the car park, so I kept saying, 'Come on, Mother,' as I do, but she kept on staring. So I went to investigate. She'd been nosing at a tall, dark, handsome fella bonking the life out of a real smart blonde woman in the back of a car. I couldn't believe it! So I said again, 'Come on, Mother. Move yourself,' and she simply replied, 'Hang on a minute, love, he's nearly on the glory stroke.' I just died. I told her to behave herself but she simply told me to chill out again. Then we just sat in the car. 'Well I never,' she said. 'You should have seen the weapon on him; it was like a pensioner's leg!'

Honestly, I couldn't cope sometimes, and then she'd go on to say, 'If I was only forty years younger.' God help me!

I have two brothers and I often look back and remember her saying, 'Do you know, my greatest wish is for all my boys to get on.' That's a tall order. I can never see that happening. Her favourite saying was, 'It's nice to be important, but it's more important to be nice.' My God, she loved that one. Another she would say was, 'You can live with someone for fifty years and you still don't know them.' She always told me, 'Have a go at your family but nobody else's.' Just like Les Dawson having a go at his mother-in-law.

The times I had to play the piano for her to sing were too many to count. She sometimes even developed an American accent! She could be so over the top. I couldn't work it out back then... but I now know where I get it from!

She would never consent to visiting her parents' grave. It was as if they had never existed. And now that I'm virtually without a family I find, like my mother, I can't go to her and

Dad's grave. When I drive past I turn my head as if there's nothing there. I just can't face it. I refuse to acknowledge they are gone. It's almost like I've just not seen them for a while.

Planet Margaret

Like the focal point in any Welsh home, the parlour (*y parlwr*) housed the china cabinet. This was a big thing in my mother's life and she kept her mother's best china in it. My word, it was a fine piece of furniture. I still have the bone china, tea and coffee pots, crystal glasses and vases, etc. Anything and everything of value would go in the china cabinet... which leads me to my next story.

My mother was in her shop, or should I say on stage, and a frail, elderly lady from across the road came over to buy some goods. The old lady asked for a pound of potatoes and said to make them big ones. A bit tight you might well say! Well, she ended up with two spuds, and my mother said, 'I bet she puts them in her china cabinet!'

She was such a shrewd businesswoman, but then she pleaded poverty at all times, too. I won't tell you how much she left me. My God! But she had simple needs. Her shop was her saviour and her chapel was her real home. She loved her car and enjoyed going to bingo with her friends. I cannot imagine what my life would be like if I hadn't had a mother like mine. I would probably be in a 9-to-5 job and would never have seen 16 countries.

She pushed me as if it was her duty in life. Showbusiness was so important to her, and she lived her life through me. She would tell me that showbusiness was the only business that could allow you to mix with royalty, politicians and the ordinary folk on the street. She had no family of her own; she was an only child and was only eight years old when her mother died. That was a massive pain for her to bear.

I have to admit, I can't imagine me popping back and fore to my brothers' houses now. It's gone too far for me, sad as it sounds. When something dies it cannot be revived. I don't even know their phone numbers. I'm just so glad that I have Gabe and my godson, Sam. Like my mother, I love to give and we always got a big kick out of giving.

My mother would sometimes slip off into cloud cuckoo land. She'd start fantasising and come out with belters to people like, 'Oh, our Chris has got a new girlfriend. There's hope for me to have grandchildren yet.' I'd know what was happening. She was on Planet Margaret again... but I just let her get on with it. I have to admit that I have never been out with a girl in my life. I'd have to read the instructions and would probably have to have a gun held to my head. 'It's not too late,' she would say, and I would always have to say something like, 'Mother, dream on!'

She had so many clothes. I would say she had about half a dozen sets of different sized clothes as she was always on diets... I suppose a bit like Oprah Winfrey (so I've read!) I think now I dress a bit outrageously sometimes, especially on stage – always black and bling – and if my mother was still here she would say, as she always did, 'You can't beat a pair of Cuban heels and a double vent at the back of your jacket, because you are stocky and a foot and a fart.' That's what she would say. I always wanted to wear way-out clothes but there was an air of disapproval about this from Her Royal Cwmafan-ness!

I suppose that it was a bit like *Billy Elliot* in our house with my mother pushing me with the arts and my father wanting me to be a rough and ready lad. I always felt a bit of a disappointment to my father, but towards the end he really did understand me and he really did love Gabe. My mother worshipped the ground that Gabe walked on and she loved to see him pop in on his own. They were great friends.

Seldom did I receive disapproval in my choice of friends, but my taking Lavina Smith home did cause ructions. I had just planned to drop by to see her in Cardiff, but her husband had taken the car to work and she desperately wanted to go shopping. So when I called she asked me if I was going shopping. I said that I was but I was going to see my mother for an hour first. Well, off we went and we got to Cwmafan, I opened my mother's door and introduced Lavina to her. Immediately she looked at the lady friend of mine and said, 'Who is she? And where's my Gabe?' It was like I was wrong to have a woman at my side and God help that she was only tagging along to go shopping with me. Gabe was firmly set in stone and that was that. Even my father was good with Gabe. But what can you do? I wasn't going to change.

Back then we had something else in common. We both lived for our cigs and she loved to have foreign cigarettes and to show them off big style at the bingo. She would say, 'Our Chris has brought these back from his trips abroad.' Oh, how she loved to pose and flash things in front of people. I think it was just to make her feel important.

Her love for children was immense and I often wonder what she would have been like if she'd known Sam. If ever they showed starving children on the television, it would set her off. She couldn't help but start to cry. Sam's the same when he sees the advert with abused children in it. He tells his dad to turn it over because he gets really upset.

My mother's faith was incredible too and I often heard her praying in different places. She was totally devoted to the Lord and that was that. No exceptions! I really do believe that she couldn't have got through her life without her faith.

And she loved to laugh. She had a data bank of jokes that were incredible and more often than not they were usually about my father. She had her favourites and could not help repeating them, and often, too. She always took the mick out of my father. She'd say, 'He's just like the dog when it comes to Welsh. He understands it but can't speak it!' Here are just a few of her tales:

If my father was undressing near the bedroom window my mother would say, 'Come away from that window, otherwise people will think I've married you for your money!'

Or there's the one about Gladys and Dai in bed. Gladys says to Dai, 'Will you nibble my ear like you used to in the old days?' and Dai would reply, 'Go to sleep, Gladys. By the time I find my teeth it will be morning.'

However, with my mother, it was always 'My Chris' or 'My number one'. The relationship we had was mega special. Nothing would, nor could, get between us. We were so similar in our ways and it was sometimes hard living up to her expectations, but I managed it – most of the time! I'd only have to play the piano and she'd melt. I think she wanted to look like Pamela Anderson, and flaunt her attributes wherever she went. She was certainly a handful. I often wonder how my father put up with it all.

My mother was always 'on stage', and loved to put my dad in his place. I remember her telling some women in the village that my father had to give the Post Office some ID to cash his pension, and that one day he'd forgotten his ID so he decided to show his grey, hairy chest to prove his age. And then she would come out with the punchline. She'd say, 'Harold, you should have shown the post mistress your old boy; you could have claimed disability, then!'

I remember years ago going to Cardiff with my mother to buy stuff for the shop, and we went for a meal in a nice restaurant. As usual, my mother ordered a ham salad as she was 'still' on a diet, and when the meal came she took one bite of the ham and shrieked. I asked her, 'What's the matter?' and she simply answered, 'Fetch that bloody

waitress!' So I did. The waitress asked what was wrong
and my mother turned the slice of ham over and there was
mustard on it, as if the ham had come off another plate.
My mother said, 'You dirty cow,' and threw the ham at the
waitress. 'You eat it!' she said. On the way out she said to the
waitress, 'I've got contacts. You'll be on *News at Ten* tonight.'
Then she stood outside the restaurant telling everyone going
in about what had happened. Lots of people turned away
and went somewhere else. What a girl!

One time she was in her car waiting to pull out of a
junction, and was a bit slow off the mark. The man behind
was becoming very impatient and eventually he got out of
his car and tapped her window and said to her, 'Thinking of
moving today, lady?' She closed the window, got out of the
car, locked it, put the alarm on and said, 'Up yours, baby. I'm
going shopping,' and off she went. She called a policeman
and told him she'd broken down and that the man behind
was harassing her. The man had long gone but she had
taken his registration number and he was warned not to
harass sweet old ladies. That's my girl!

My mother had bags of confidence. She never thought
twice about anything because she was always right. And
who would be brave enough to tell her anything different?
She was really confident, even when coming through
customs on the way home from Belgium. In those days you
were only allowed to bring 200 cigs back home. She had
fags in her handbag, inside a pair of knickers, single packets
in her bra, and even in some toys that our Belgium family
had bought us to come back home. I had a dumper truck
in a posh box and I was told by my mother to carry it and
not to let any strange man touch it, and if the customs man
asked to see it, I was to start screaming. Mind you, it never
got that far. The customs man asked, 'What's in there, son?
Can I have a look?' and I said, 'No, it's mine.' He replied,
'Okay, fair enough.' But my mother saw no danger, and as

she walked through customs she said to my father, 'See, they don't do their jobs properly. I'd never give them a job!'

If my mother was in a shop somewhere, and the assistant was a bit slow or talking, she would say, 'Excuse me, my dear. Sorry to trouble you when you are working, but if you don't mind… ' Or she'd say, 'If you don't mind, I've got a husband to cook supper for.'

I once sat with my mother watching the TV and there was a documentary on about IVF treatment. It was all about a woman who wanted to have a baby and had tried unsuccessfully for fifteen years. I was only young and didn't really understand the situation but I do remember my mother saying, 'Bloody hell, your father would only have to take his trousers off and that would be it!'

Time to move on

It's been nearly ten years since my mother's death, and how am I? I don't know how to put this into words, but I'll try. 'Did I do enough?' is what keeps coming back to haunt me. Although my mother was very liberal, did I disappoint her by being gay? Could she cope with the fact that she had a poofter for a son in a small Welsh village? Did she cope with that fact? Did she hide it sometimes?

I think sometimes I might have, as she wanted grandchildren like she needed oxygen. I wake some mornings and I forget that she's dead, and I go to phone her and have to stop in my tracks as the truth hits me again, as if I was reliving that dreadful day. I wanted to tell her so much more about the real me; my feelings and my ambitions. She probably knew most of them but I still feel as if I was robbed.

I have to bite my lip when people say to me that they've lost their parent at the age of 92 or something, but there you go. Good luck to them. I mean that sincerely, especially if they had all those extra years. How I envy them. My mother loved life so much and I remember worrying about her just after my father died. I was leaving the house to go back to Cardiff and she was in a state. I knew she wanted me to stay but I had to get back to work, and see to my flat and so on, and I said to her, 'Mammy, will you be alright for me to go?' And she said, very convincingly, 'I'll be okay, don't worry. I love life too much to do anything silly.'

I start to remember things; it's like having flashbacks. Her talking about things like silent heart attacks. What was that all about? Maybe I should have been more up front with the doctor and questioned him more? Could I have prolonged her life? I keep asking myself over and over. Maybe I could have been a better son? I remember the night before she died, she wanted to speak to me on the phone. We spoke for a good while but then I hurried her up as I was tired and I had people round the flat. How did she feel when I put the phone down? Nobody expects their mother to die tomorrow at the age of 66.

I wonder what life would be like if my mother was still alive? My brothers would probably be speaking to me and I'd be having fun spoiling my nieces and nephews. But alas, it's not like that at all. The trouble all started with the will, as it does with most families. My mother left everything to me and I couldn't help that. I think, given time, I would have done something nice with it all, but life isn't like that for me. The trouble and damage that the will caused has been immeasurable and it's not been my fault.

At the time of the reading of the document I was so hurt and so destroyed at the loss of my mother that the will did not interest me. I did then say that I would love for the house to stay in the family, and that maybe one of the children would live in it. But there are lots of children in the family. So that's all said. I was not going to do what my mother did and leave it or sign it over to only one. If

I were to leave it, in whatever shape, it would have to be between *all* of the children, and not just one, causing more friction. Now, you'd think that would be welcomed and seen to be fair. But with my family? No way. From then on there was silence – well, after all the recriminations – but since? Nothing. No speaking. Nothing! So I've left it to Gabe. That was my decision and that's that. And as for the rest? Well, there's a bit of mistletoe hanging from the tail of my shirt!

But, given time, we all reflect on the past and decisions change. Goalposts move. And I realise that I need to move on from all of this. There's nothing I can do to bring her back, I know. The house is not my mother, and it can never replace her. I have decided that perhaps I now *need* to sell the house. It should go to a family that will make it live again with children, instead of me keeping it as a shrine. I am confused, but I have to sort myself out. I'm so bloody good at giving advice to others but do I do the right thing for me? No, not at all. I no longer feel that there's ever going to be a reconciliation with the rest of my family, so I might as well sell up, do a runner and start up a new life with Gabe somewhere in the sun.

I now know that I have to leave Wales, as at times it's so depressing, with the wind and the rain and the floods, the constant restrictions and new laws, and official decisions that seem to be accepted without thought or consultation. Nobody should have to put up with it. There are places that are always sunny and I long to go to and see these places before I die. If I do die here, I want my ashes to be scattered in Spain, because if you do come back again, it has to be somewhere hot.

Really, life is too short and I'm not fretting any more. I did for a while, but no more! One thing that comes from this is that I can sleep at night knowing I'd done right by my mother, I always did what she asked of me and I know I was adored by her.

My hero

If I had three wishes, firstly I'd want my health to be good, and Gabe's as well. Secondly, I'd wish it was nearing the time for me to move elsewhere. And thirdly I'd wish I had a child. I'm still broody.

People are forever asking me why I don't adopt a child. The trouble is, the child would never be mine, and what would I be like, years on, when he's looking for his blood parents? I couldn't hack that. I look at Madonna out in Africa and adopting children. I think it's wonderful what she does, but I want *my own* child so desperately.

I have to admit that my godson Sam has helped to fill this gap. Seeing that I've known him since a wee baby and now he's heading towards being five, the love I have for him is so real that he could be my child. I don't think I could stop loving him. I love him as much as I would my own flesh and blood and, if I couldn't see him again, that would finish me. So I've got to resolve myself to the fact that I'm never going to have a child of my own. But I have my Sammy, and he is the total world to me. He's mine and I'll always be there for him.

Well, what can I say? He's my hero. He's calmed me right down, and he's so famous that when people meet his father, Bruce Anderson, they ask him, 'Are you Sammy's father?' Famous child or what! I long to see him and he heals me. He makes me feel content, and I couldn't imagine my life without him. At the age of four he started talking like an eight year old. He's so advanced that it's spooky, but then his parents talk to him like an adult. We never speak down to him. As I always say, I feel I am the chosen one as far as he is concerned, because of his acceptance.

Recently I hadn't seen him for a fortnight, so I arranged to call over and we gave each other the biggest hug ever. He told me all about his holiday in Tenerife and about the food and, of course, his love of the water. I was so looking forward to seeing him in his school uniform. I don't want him to grow up! We'd all love him to stay at age four – not just me – but Sam was ready for the big school from the moment he went to see it. He was so excited and now he loves it. He looks so smart in his uniform and is always chatting about all the new friends he has made.

I love it when he calls me 'Chris Needs', full title, as does Gabe's mam. When I arrive back home after work, I look at his photographs everywhere about the place and I wish I could pop into his room to see him sleeping, and watch him move about when he has a dream. I drop in with his comics and usually they are full of stickers. God help his mother's fridge!

Sam is so advanced it's really quite incredible. I know everyone says their child is the best, but this little one is on his own! His love for music is immense and he often requests different songs in the car with his dad. I remember calling to see him one day and Sam was upstairs in his mam and dad's room watching TV. I shouted up to him, 'Are you coming down?' and he replied, 'In a minute, this programme's nearly finished.' So I crept upstairs and there he was, lying on the big bed, and he simply pressed pause on the remote control. So I said to him, 'How do you know which button is the pause button?' and he said back to me, 'Oh, Chris Needs, it's the button with the number 11 on it,' (which is the sign, of course, for 'pause' on these handsets).

He is growing up so fast and I sometimes wish I could freeze time. He's perfect just as he is. What do I see him doing when he grows up? I just don't know. This little one is going to surprise us all, I think, but music is a favourite, I know. I wouldn't like to see him 'doing the clubs' but maybe presenting (perhaps at the BBC?), or travelling the world working in tourism. I don't know, but whatever his love is going to be, I'll be there to support and guide him. He's my boy! I bet if my mother was still alive she would spoil Sammy rotten, too.

Why I could never come back to Cwmafan to live

My mother only wanted to live in Rhos, near Pontardawe. That was her all-time ambition and she often drove there and studied some of the properties. She had her head in the clouds just like me. A chip off the old block, you might say. Maybe I should have moved her permanently to Cardiff, next door to me. Perhaps by not being so lonely, and having Gabe and I just next door, she would have lived a bit longer? I really do think she died of a broken heart, and I probably shall, too.

Things come back to me about my mother; things that happened in the days when money was short. I remember her going without for me to have piano lessons. Was it to be a game of bingo or was she to pay for my piano lessons? You can guess which one won! But I can remember her saying to me, 'They'll all have a bloody shock after my days.' And I always said the expected thing back, 'Oh, Mother, stop being so morbid.' But then the will did eventually come out and you might say that the mucky stuff hit the air cooling perambulator.

What would she say about the state of the world today? Probably what Catherine Tate says: 'What a load of old f***ing shit!' And she'd not be too far wrong. She wanted at one time to stand for Parliament. The Tory of all Tories, believe you me. I think she might have made a difference.

I also remember her saying to me, 'I know you'll never come back here to live.' And I answered by saying, 'You'll never know.' But, once again, she was spot on. No, I couldn't go back to Cwmafan permanently. Too many bad memories of the abuse. And when in town I'd probably see the family of this man walking about, and I couldn't stand that. Who's the one that got away with this? Not me! I wanted to reveal the name of the man who did all those awful things, but then I'd destroy other innocent people's lives. So I didn't, even though mine was destroyed. Then I wanted to tell his next of kin about what happened, but was that the right thing to do? No. I believe that I should have tried to tell my parents, but that was not possible way back then. I would have been punished for all that.

I remember once my mother asking me what had happened to my neck. Had I hurt myself in gym in school? I said I had and she was going to go to the school to put the gym teacher right, and adding that she wasn't happy about me having rope burns on my neck. Little did she know that I had tried to hang myself in the toilets with the leather strap from my satchel and it had snapped (cheap, again) and just grazed my neck. It was hard being called a 'queer' and other names, and having no support from the teachers. At times the other kids in school were absolutely frightening. You'd never believe how glad I was to get out of that institution. And my mother never knew about that incident.

I think if my mother was here today she would tell me that I am too much of an open book. She always pleaded poverty but left me an absolute fortune: ground, property, policies, cash everywhere and savings accounts galore. She would hide money in the tumble drier and in socks in the drawer, and if I ever wanted something like a car (and she was car mad), she'd say, 'Of course you should have that car. You might be dead a week Wednesday,' and send me upstairs to get a thousand pounds or two and tell me not to tell my father. Then at other times my father would come up to me and say, 'Put this money away on top of the wardrobe, or under the stairs, and don't show your mother.' It was all confusing, but they worked so hard and gave me everything from pianos to money to open the Tower Hotel.

She used to come out with lines that would make your hair stand on end. I remember us watching *Miss World* and this gorgeous young girl walked on the set with next to nothing on and with a figure to die for. My mother looked at her and said, 'If I had a figure like that I wouldn't be serving in that bloody shop over the road, let me tell you.' I sometimes think my mother would have liked to have been an escort, and live the high life in penthouse flats with rich businessmen. She just wanted to be noticed. As I said before, her own mother died when she was just eight, and I try to think back to see how she coped with the loss. I think she suffered more than me. She never ever got over the loss.

There is definitely a big hole in my life and I believe that it's a new life that I'm living as the old one has gone. I have to bear the pain every day as I think of my mother constantly. My God, I don't know where I'd be without Gabe. Probably in some corner, out of my head. He definitely gives me stability and keeps a check on me now that my mother's gone. I think back to the year 2000, when she died, and how I felt then. I thought then that I would never be able to do anything again as long as I lived. I felt as if the end of the world had come and I had no idea what to do. But today, all I can say is that I try. Some days are worse than others and some days are bearable. Yes, it is a new life and I'm not always fussed on it. Sometimes the clouds part, and the sun comes shining through, but not often enough.

And so, decisions have to be made. At last I can do it. I have to downsize my life and accept these are my decisions, my choices. But where to begin? Mother, I have to start in Cwmafan.

I was recently listening to BBC Radio Wales when a favourite programme of mine came on, called *The Final Curtain*, with the one and only Max Boyce. It's a one-to-one chat show in which guests talk about their last requests. This edition in particular was really good, with the brilliant

songstress Rebecca Evans from Pontrhydyfen. She said
that she was honoured that her village had recognised her
by placing her name on its welcome sign. I was, and am,
genuinely pleased for Rebecca. But somehow I felt I couldn't
imagine Cwmafan doing that for me. In fact at that time I'd
have put a small fortune on it. Mind you, I did get abusive
symbols and comments painted on my mother's garage
door; a number of 'Fs' and 'Cs' to add to the bad taste.

Happier memories of village life

On a lighter note, there were many good times too, but
I often have difficulty in recalling these memories until
something trivial triggers them off.

Every Monday morning in school I used to buy saving
stamps. There were green ones with Princess Anne on
them for 9d, and blue ones with Prince Charles on them.
They were 2/6 (half a crown). I was so proud of my saving
skills back then. I wish I was now but I'm too much of a
shopaholic! One day while walking to school, I got as far as
Cunard Terrace, only about two blocks away (you can tell
I've been to America!), where they have no front gardens,
and walked straight out of their houses onto the pavement.
I stopped in my tracks and turned around as I thought I had
left my savings money and the book to stick the stamps in
at home. Back I went and it was a windy day, blowing a gale
right up the valley. I must have got about 100 yards and then
realised that they were in my back pocket all the time... so
I turned around and headed back to school. As I did, the
slates flew off the roof of one of the houses a couple of yards
in front of me and came crashing down on the pavement. I
felt sick, as I knew that if I hadn't turned back I would have
been a goner. So you see it's good to save; especially for
your old age. I'm not that much of a saver. People say that I
should save like hell for my old age. And I keep telling them,

my savings have got me this far!

My paper round has to be something that should go down in history. Everybody I knew had a job. I didn't really want one, but if everyone else had one then I wanted one too. So I went to the local paper shop and spoke to the lovely Mag Richardson and she agreed to give me a paper round. The round was Heol Camlas in Tabor, Cwmafan. It was a very long street, made up of about 50 or 60 houses overlooking the Waun where I lived. I learned after a while to put the papers up blindfolded and was away to deliver them like a woman possessed. I had to wear something different every morning in case someone was up early and spotted me in the same outfit twice. Some of the people were very interesting and I made a lot of nice friends through the paper round.

One of the people living there was my mother's dear friend Mair Jinks, Richard Burton's niece. I got a fag from her every time. Tea, toast and a fag I'd have there, every morning. I always remember Myra and Roger, they were always so welcoming to me, and right at the end of the street was my friend John Miles' house and I'd be in there for hours playing records.

When I was gallivanting one day on my paper round I saw a van shaking back and fore, with all sorts of noises coming out of it. Well, I just had to have a look. After all, it was *my* street. There was this fella, quite nice looking, bonking away with a girl I knew from my school. I thought to myself, so that's how it's done and that's where you shove it. I had a good look and the fella saw me and told me to sling my hook. Mind you, she was a bit of a dog and not good looking; but him, he was lovely. He could have done better for himself, I can tell you.

I remember finding a purse on the pavement and I was going to give it in to Mrs Richardson but there was a name in it (I don't remember it now), so I took it to the lady's house and she was quite well-to-do. She was so grateful as there was a wad of notes in it and at the age of 12 I was given a tenner for my honesty. I couldn't believe it and I rushed home to tell my mother. She was flabbergasted and then looked at me with those sad eyes. Boy, she was good at that. Now these were the days when my father was a steelworker and it was *always* a struggle to make ends meet. I immediately gave the ten-pound note to my mother and the look on her face is something I'll never forget. It was like a weight was lifted from her shoulders and she was even a little teary. I felt good about what I had done and roamed the streets like a gold digger, looking downwards and hoping to find more 'luckies'.

The paper round lasted years and I loved every minute of it. I'd get Christmas bonuses galore. One year I must have had more than £25 in tips and presents. Mind you, I used to pick up fags for certain customers too. They would say to me on a Monday, 'Will you bring me ten Number 6 cigarettes and keep the change.' This I would do. I would have a few pennies left over for me in change, and then I'd give the fags to the lady or whoever. Usually they would then give me a fag from the packet to be going on with! They were such great days and I miss them. There was one fella who would ask me to take messages on the sly. He'd say, 'Tell *so and so* in number *x* not to come down until after 11 am.' I was beginning to feel like a bit of a madam!

There was never any trouble, like being mugged or robbed or anything like that, and on a Saturday morning I would collect all the money and balance the books. Not like today. I wouldn't leave the milk money out on the doorstep. Nor the milk come to that. Nor the doorstep really!

I think I found my vocation while on paper round duty. I met lots of lonely people who couldn't wait for me to push the paper through the door, and the second I did push it through, the door would open and there would be an elderly lady smiling at me and she would say, 'Cup of tea, love?' I think some of the younger women would have wanted more, if I had been a bit older and not a poof of course. But the bereaved ladies looked forward to a chat, and to making me tea and toast. So many of these lonely ladies only had me to talk to in days. It was very sad indeed.

My mother always wanted to know why my paper round would take several hours to finish, but it was all the meeting and greeting that I did. There was an old man who wanted bread and fags on a Wednesday and I was his delivery boy – and you think shopping online is the in thing. No, this was personal shopping like you get in the big department stores. You could see his bedroom windows from the back of my mother's house and on a Tuesday, if he left his top window open he wanted two packets of fags. You got to learn the various codes. I always had money spare from the odd jobs I would do here and there, either down the club or running messages. My nana was a very giving lady. Every time I went to see her I was given money, and quite a bit I hasten to add. I'd have a pound note or a load of silver. Money was plentiful for this young lad. When I finished on the paper round it was like a funeral had happened, but I still used to take fags and bread up to the old man when he left his window open. People would stop me in town and say, 'Oh, my mother misses you calling every morning.' You can see where it comes from.

I used to see a lot of domestics as well. I would push the paper through the door and if I could hear shouting, I always had a listen. One day the woman came to the door and said thanks for the paper and to excuse her as she was peeling onions. They must have thought I was born yesterday. In one particular house en route there would always be shouting, and I'd walk as slow as I could and hover next to the door pretending to fold the paper to get all the gossip and to see what was happening. I could have written a book on that house alone. It was nice doing the round and it gave me an insight to life, which comes in handy today with what I do now on the wireless.

Another job I had was in Halfords in Station Road, Port Talbot. It was a summer holiday job and I'd be on the shop floor. I had big ideas about being there and was doing quite well until one day, when the manager called me in to the back room and told me to wash the dishes and mugs and showed me how to do it. He said, 'Make sure the part where you drink from is scrubbed properly.' From that moment I went off the job straight away. I was doing the dishes for my mother every day before going to work as she hated housework big time. I was blowed if I was going to go to work and do it all over again. I eventually finished, and from the money I had made with that job I bought myself an organ which was put in pride of place in the parlour.

When Port Talbot was Port Talbot

The Beach Hill bridge has gone and I wasn't consulted. How can anyone in their right mind take away a landmark that means so much to people? I was so hurt when Betty May told me on air. Do these people not care what happens to a town or city? Port Talbot used to have a lot of character, but now I don't think it has much. Major shops have deserted us for nearby towns or out-of-town centres – those that haven't folded due to the recession. You have to go to Neath for so many things these days.

It's such a shame. I will not drive to the beach via Water Street. I just cannot see the Beach Hill not being there, if you follow my meaning. To get to Victoria Road I drive around Baglan and up the seafront, past the Four Winds and that is that. When will people learn to leave people's memories and feelings alone? All in the name of progress! Port Talbot needs to clean up its ideas, what with that awful smell lingering. Some days as I pass through Margam I have to hold my breath as it stinks of rotten eggs. The smell of sulphur from the steelworks is unbearable. No wonder I have a bad chest after all those years in that so-called school.

Somebody told me a Port Talbot joke the other day. (Forgive me, I'm only quoting!) A girl says to her boyfriend, 'Kiss me where it's wet and smelly.' So her boyfriend drove her to Port Talbot. What can I say?

Another joke: one man asks another, 'What is that yellow shiny thing up in the sky?' and his mate replies, 'I don't know. I'm from Port Talbot.'

I still can't get over the change in name from Port Talbot to Neath Port Talbot. What the hell is that all about? I went away to work and when I came back I was from a different place. I always thought Port Talbot was Port Talbot and Neath was Neath and the county was West Glamorgan. Was anyone consulted about this, or was it just another 'take it lying down again' like the smoking ban? My God, if I was still smoking there would be riots on the streets.

I'm so glad to say that there are parts of Cwmafan that still look the same as they did years ago and that pleases me. I'm still getting used to the new houses where Pelly Street was and the other new houses down by the old chemist, not far from Gatti's (*the* café of café's). There's a large piece of ground at the side of the Rolling Mill. I've often wondered if anyone will do something with that.

My mother's house was a sanctuary for all South Wales artistes. The fact that my father had a fish and chip shop was an added attraction and my musician friends often popped in for a good old feed. At the end of one summer season, two musicians I had met in Jersey told me that they would look me up in Cwmafan. One day my mother phoned to tell me that they had turned up outside the house in a massive van that they slept in. She'd explained to them that

I was in Spain but it hadn't put them off. They stayed for a good while outside the house and enjoyed the chip shop as well. Good Welsh hospitality, I suppose.

One day, when I'd returned home, Phil Chapman (a local act) and a few musicians from the Taibach Working Men's Club were in the living room in my mother's house. She popped over from the shop to have a chat with us and the house was so full that she sat on the glass coffee table. All of a sudden the glass gave way and she fell through with glass spears sticking up all around her. For a minute we all laughed, but then reality hit home and we realised that she could have died. Phil Chapman picked her out of the table and then she started to cry, having just realised that she came close to death. That was never forgotten and was brought up at times when a tragedy occurred. After that it was a wooden table and a lot of reminiscing.

CHAPTER THREE

Working the Clubs

Thrown to the lions

WHEN I BOUGHT THE organ that was the start of clubland. Starting out was hard! My first booking was in the Waun Club in Cwmafan and I found it really difficult. I was really thrown to the lions. Older, experienced artistes walked in and threw sheet music at me, expecting me to sound like an orchestra, which of course I didn't. A lot of the artistes were quite horrible. Fortunately one or two were really encouraging. I took everything that was said to heart and sometimes I really wanted to give the lot up. It was strange becoming a professional musician. There was a code of conduct, so to speak, to learn and it grew on me. Before long I had learned enough to cope on my own out in the big wide world of pianists.

After many successful years as an accompanist I tried my hand at being the 'act' on the stage. I always felt out of the equation by being a musician and thought things would have been better as an artiste. The first booking I ever did was in Port Talbot and there was an organist there ready to play for me. Now, I had written all my music myself perfectly and I knew every dot on the page. The organist looked a bit nervous about playing for me and said, 'I thought you would be playing for yourself.' When I walked on stage he started to play. Trust me, it resembled nothing that was on the paper. I couldn't believe that someone could play so badly (you can thank me later for not naming you) and my face must have said it all. I took hold of the music and threw it off stage. The organist ran off to the wings thinking it was a joke and came back on to play for me once again. When he returned, I was sat on the organ playing for myself. I simply said to him, 'I've taken your advice. You've convinced me to play for myself.' He thought he had done me a favour, and to be honest he had. He thought that he was the Welsh version of Liberace, but he sounded more like Les Dawson with his playing out of tune.

One time I was working in the valleys and when I arrived there was another act on with me. This girl was so up her own arse, it was unbelievable. She told me of things she'd done in London, and the big shows abroad, and the radio work, etc. She went on blowing her own trumpet. She had some nice songs but I could see disaster looming. She approached the organist and said that she wanted this one like this, and the other one like that, and then the organist said, 'Let me tell you what I know and see if you can sing any of them.' He didn't read music, nor could he play more than half a dozen songs!

She went on stage and died a death. Then it was my turn and, boy, was I rubbing my hands. I walked on stage, sat at the keyboard and started off with some Billy Joel and then some Elton John. She was pig sick and, boy, did she eat humble pie when I came off. She begged me to play for her, otherwise she was going to be paid off. I could see that she had learnt a big lesson that night so I did play for her and she did a bomb. Good backing is everything. We are still, from time to time, in touch to this very day and she often reminds me how bloody stupid she was. And I often tell her how right she is.

I was probably one of the top three organists in the 1970s and met so many acts. If the singer rubbed me up the wrong way I used to get my own back by altering the pitch of the organ and making them sound flat or, even worse, sharp. The customers in the club would never suspect me of playing badly. I was their boy; their number one. Maybe what I did was wrong but it was poetic justice, and while I was destroying the act I used to think, 'Take me to court, you clever bugger.'

After some years of doing a great job, and only destroying the dickheads, my reputation went before me. Even the acts from the North East that came down for a couple of weeks' work knew that the backing in the Taibach 'workies' was the best. I was offered loads of jobs and took one offer up at the White Wheat in Maesteg, which I loved dearly. I was resident at the Bryngelli Country Club which then became Ford's and is now the Visteon Club. That was a great place and I made a lot of fans in Swansea through performing there. It was all well and good being the power behind the act but it was the 'behind' that I didn't like. I wanted to be out front receiving the flowers and the accolades.

The age of Aquarius

I remember passing my driving test when I was 17. The minister, Ronald Williams, was with me at the time and I was up for an audition for keyboard player with a Swansea-based group called Aquarius. So off I toddled, full of confidence in my orange mini, all the way from Cwmafan. I got there and went in for the audition. The group consisted of Barry Haynes on drums, his wife Aileen on lead vocals and her brothers Phil, on guitar and Reg on bass. It was quite a family affair. For the audition I was asked to play the organ, back an act and then play with the group.

To this day I remember Barry's reaction to my playing. He said, 'How old are you?' When I said 'Seventeen' he replied, 'Jesus, amazing!' After the audition I was made to wait for the answer – was it yes or no? I popped over to the

Townsman Club later in the week to see if I could find out anything. I remember saying to Aileen, 'Excuse me, Mrs Haynes, have you any news for me?' She told me to ask the boys in the band. Later that night they came over to me and told me that the job was mine, and I was delighted. I felt as if I had made it.

The band's family was based in Pineda de Mar, Spain, and they asked me to go with them for three weeks. I thought it would be nice to go as we were paid holiday money in those days by the Townsman, and so I went with them. I have to be honest, I was the biggest pain in the arse going. I moaned and groaned about everything (can you believe that?) and I'm sure that if they hadn't thought so much of me they would have told me to sling my hook. But they didn't. They realised that I was young, was very inexperienced and had an issue... with my sexuality.

Back in Swansea they tried to get me to open up about being gay, but I wouldn't as I thought I would be picked on by other staff in the Townsman. We are talking 1972 here. Things were much different then. Trust me. To be honest, I never really opened up to them and they had the consideration to leave it where it was, on the shelf somewhere.

I can honestly say that they all truly loved me like another brother, and they also got on brilliantly with my family. As I write this, I have sad feelings as some have passed on. I don't make enough effort to see them and this I must do. So, boys and girls, if you are reading this, I'm sorry that I haven't been in contact. But my love for you is still as massive as ever. (Private joke: Reg, you're so vain.)

Backing some big names

This very special club, the Townsman, was the first place I earned real money: forty quid a week. I gave my mother

twenty and I managed on twenty. This is where I met
Bonnie Tyler, or 'Gaynor' as we knew her. The Wignals were
the owners of the club. Believe you me, they were so very
good to me. In particular Derek Wignal. Derek would say to
me, 'Come on, Chris, let's all go for a curry,' and he would
take us out, or take me over to the casino. Boy, I felt like I
was in Monte Carlo. It was all so very exciting. I used to see
the big businessmen from Swansea out on the town with
their bits of stuff and spending a small fortune on the tables.
It was a world that was a million miles away for me and I
never ventured anywhere near.

What about all the artistes I backed? It was showbiz in
my face and it was all wondrous. I didn't sing much at that
time, as I didn't have the confidence. That came later. But
I backed loads of cabaret artistes, believe you me: Faith
Brown, Little and Large, Dana; the list was endless and I got
to know people with big names.

I remember Roger Whittaker walking into the club and
he and Derek having words about times of appearance,
and the fee, and on and on and on went the discussions!
There were many stars walking through the doors of the
Townsman, but I had a real soft spot for Marilyn, the girl
who worked on the cigarette kiosk. She used to thump men
that took the mick out of me and, boy, did she protect me
big time. She worked her way up to manager of Barons, as
it was later called. I still see her from time to time and I still
think she's ace.

While working at the Townsman, the management
opened a new club in Aberafan called the Sandman Club,
right on the seafront. Aquarius, which by this time included
me, was asked to be the resident band. I loved the idea as
I lived in Port Talbot and had less travelling to do, but of
course the others had to drive from Swansea every night.
Luck of the draw I guess. Anyway, as it was a new club it got
the cream of the artistes to set it off with a bang. I was now

very glad that I had a good amount of experience under my belt, as many big names were soon on their way to be under the command of my fingers.

One of the first artistes I ever played for was a guy I'd never heard of. His name was David Alexander. I remember him walking in with his music in a case and when he opened it, I saw he had a bottle of Aramis aftershave. I asked him if I could try it as I had never smelt it before. Straight away he said I could and I was quite smitten with the bottle, and him, to be honest. We turned into good chums and sometimes he would insist on me playing for him, which was a good thing for me to have on my CV. He sang great songs like 'Hickory Hollers Tramp' and 'The Rhondda' and lots of Tom Jones songs. He went down well everywhere he went. Fond memories, I have to admit.

One other artiste I really fell for was Anita Harris. She pinched our bandroom because it was bigger, but I didn't mind as I was a bit star-struck with her. She treated me wonderfully and gave me great compliments about my playing. My mother and father came to see Anita singing at the Sandman and they had a front table right on the cabaret floor. I told Anita where my parents were and during her act she went straight to them and said, 'Hello, Margaret,' and then, 'Hello, Harold, have you come straight from work?' Then we realised that my father still had his muddy shoes on from the allotment and my mother nearly battered him. I mean, how could she ever use her posh telephone voice again after an incident like that? The week ended and I was quite sad when Anita Harris left. It's quite strange but I was listening to her being interviewed on the radio recently. You think you know everything about a person, especially when they are in the limelight, but she revealed her own torments and really seems to have been through the mill, to say the least. I'd love to ask her to do one of my variety shows.

There was always a commotion about the PA system (the

audio equipment, etc), and when one act appeared, Polly
Brown from Pickettywitch, we couldn't hear her when she
sang. Admittedly she had a quiet voice, but we just could not
hear her when the entire band was playing. After that a new
PA was put in straight away. I had a cassette tape recorder
and I taped every act I played for and guess what? I still
have them! David Alexander, Anita Harris, the lot. Even The
Peddlers and Paper Lace... eBay comes to mind, ha ha!

It was back in 1972 that I met Sue. As a singer she was
very 'soul'. We hit it off big time and were inseparable. We
went abroad together and if the backing was bad and I was
on a night off, I would play for her. Sue would come up to
my parents' house a lot and my mother and father truly
loved her. When my mother died she organised the buffet at
the funeral, and just about everything for me. When I had a
birthday bash she would organise that as well. She even got
a job on Radio Wales for a while, and after she finished we
lost touch for some reason. You know what it's like. If you
leave it too long, it's difficult to pick up the phone and just
pick up where you left off. I do miss her, truth be known. I
moved. She got married. She moved. I hope one day we'll
bump into each other and once again put the world to
rights. Just as we did before, many years ago.

One of my favourite acts ever has to be Diane Cousins.
She was a big name performing throughout Wales, an act
with great comedy and a fab voice. I was only a teenager at
the time but she turned into a true friend, and I mean that
in the every sense of the word.

In fact she was like a Sharon Osbourne figure to me in
showbusiness. She looked after me, especially when I went
to Jersey – so we are fast-forwarding some ten years here.
In 1982 I was offered a summer season in Jersey at the
Hawaiian show. When all the acts on the island went to the
Grand Hotel for the welcoming bash, lo and behold, there
was Diane representing Caesar's Palace. I felt good, I had

a friend on the island and our relationship grew from then onwards.

She once offered me a job to be her musical director and travel the world with her, but I had this bee in my bonnet about wanting to be out front and not stuck behind a keyboard making others look good, so I turned her down. I'm sorry in a strange way now, to be honest, as I think that Diane would have been good for me. She even offered to buy me a top-of-the-range keyboard, but I couldn't be persuaded. Diane remains one of my all-time favourite artistes, as well as a dear friend.

CHAPTER FOUR

The Tower

Mein host

I USED TO WORK in Jersey in the Channel Islands. I always
went over for the summer seasons and that's when I met
my first fella. As always, things were great in the beginning
but after a year or two it all went wrong. We parted but
I still was in love with Jersey. There was a pull from that
little island and it kept drawing me back. The price of the
cigarettes alone was enough to make me move in!

I started work in the Waikiki bar at the Hawaiian show
in Portelet Bay. I was soon moved into the main show as
the people who came into the bar were enjoying themselves
so much that they didn't want to go in to see the big show.
The management weighed it all up and soon I was doing
both places every night. I still get people calling me now on
the radio who used to come and see me all those years ago.
That's me: once seen never forgotten! (Gabe and myself still
like to spend time in Jersey. However, my favourite place
has to be Benidorm and my shows out there go well. But if I
could do a show anywhere in the world it would have to be
at the London Palladium. One day, perhaps?)

I came back from Jersey with my then partner and we
wanted to run our own place, with him behind the bar and
me entertaining. It was okay for the first few months. My
mam and dad helped finance us and we were on our way.

Let me describe the Tower Hotel. It's a bar, restaurant and bed and breakfast situated in Jersey Marine, about three miles from Swansea. It has a camera obscura in its grounds and is surrounded by golf courses and factories. I fancied the Tower as it had potential for a stage to put entertainment on. I built a small stage with a PA system and an electric piano. I booked acts there and I was 'mein host'.

I camped it up something rotten. Lorry drivers, parties of women, flocks of gays, they all trundled in, and as they walked in I would insult them. To a lorry driver I'd say things like, 'Thrown you out again, has she?' Or if an old lady walked in on her own I would say, 'Just come in for a warm, have you love?' Or if I really felt daring I would say to a fella with a hairy chest, 'I hate a man with a hairy chest – irritates my back terrible, it does!' The crowd would be in stitches.

The Tower was very busy. As it was out in the sticks a little, it soon became known as a place to meet. A lot of clandestine couples would book a room for a night and leave after just a few hours, saying they had to leave as something had cropped up. Yeah, I bet it had! I'd call Pat Huxtable, a lovely lady from the village and a good friend, and ask her to strip the bed. I'd tell her, 'Make sure you use rubber gloves, and put the washing machine on a boil wash, and don't sit on the bed having a fag. After all, we don't want any more babies around here now, do we?' Read the press, anything could happen!

The brewery were okay, but they gave me the odd headache with restrictions, like where I could buy my stock. And if I ran out of beer I had to get it through them only. I couldn't just nip around the corner and buy a barrel. So I had to be quite 'on the case' when ordering. But the trouble was, there was no system to the customers. I could be full on a Saturday and quiet in the week, or sometimes it would be full to the roof on a Tuesday and half a dozen in on a Saturday. Reasons for this? Well, the village might be away for a wedding. But it was generally well supported, so thanks for that.

There was plenty of room in the grounds for coaches and cars, and that helped a lot. Sometimes men with guns would come onto the grounds and start shooting birds and rabbits. I would go mental and run after them with a saucepan. Ten men with guns and me with a saucepan! I had that one from my mother. I would tell them to clear off... well, it ended in 'off' anyway! I just thought what they were doing was horrific. But I was fortunate inasmuch as my staff became great friends. Apart from Pat Huxtable, in the early days at the Tower there was her daughter-in-law, Linda, and a girl from Port Tennant called Nancy. Oh boy, I loved Nancy and still do, dearly!

However, my partner and I grew apart. Or should I say, he grew apart from me. It was very hurtful and I got very suspicious; so much so that I once flew to his home as he was there visiting his family. I turned up and he said that there was someone else, and that I meant nothing to him. I was devastated, and returned back to the Tower. He came back, but he didn't pull his weight. He pulled other things, as in other men. He would disappear in the car, but got caught out in the end. He kept bringing a young boy into the bar, or a new friend just turned up at the hotel, unannounced, to see him. It came to an abrupt end with me asking him to leave, and my staying and becoming the licensee.

It was all too much to bear. I watched him leave and fell to the floor, heartbroken. I phoned my mother and told her he had gone. She legged it over from Cwmafan and started to pick up the pieces that were strewn in front of her. I was absolutely finished, but my mother saved my life. She moved in and helped run the bar, cooked meals and looked after me.

I had to go to court and apply to become the licensee and I'm glad to say it was quite straightforward. But it was a very disturbing time for me and my parents, and I only got through it with help from my friends. I was lucky with booking artistes as I knew so many of them and I could just phone them up and book them direct at *my* place. I remember one New Year's Eve, after the ex had left. I was very down, and I tried to carry on like a good entertainer but I must have upset one woman (and not a nice one at that) from Jersey Marine village because she ran a trip over to the next pub which left me empty. Would I expect anything less? What surprised me was that almost all the village followed her. They probably didn't have minds of their own. Do I care? Not in the least. I'm just looking back at some of the depressing bits. They are still there, in the past. But look at me now; I am flying!

The Tower came to an end because it was too difficult to run on my own. I was not enjoying life, or the stigma of '*him*' and the nasty comments from locals. I just had to leave, but I had nowhere to go. I asked my mother if I could come home, but that was too difficult as she said it would cause friction with my brothers. So I bought a house in Briton Ferry. It was a really nice house but I was so lonely, so I sold it more or less straight away. I rented a flat in Swansea but that turned out to be like being put in a home. The landlord lived on the premises and would not allow me to have guests in after a certain time. I soon told him to shove his flat up his arse (sideways)!

When I left the Tower, I started receiving threatening letters from my ex-partner. I still have them, but you learn after a while… most people are full of shit.

I decided I didn't want to be part of a war so I made my plans. When I bought the contents of the Tower I also bought a painting of the establishment dated 1891 – a wonderful watercolour of the hotel, set back from the dunes with day-trippers in Victorian costume paddling on the beach. I have been bombarded with offers for it, but I've never sold it. I have it now to this day. Bittersweet memories.

The Tower is still up and running and the new people have done it proud. I went to a wedding there once and it was like walking into wonderland. Boy, it felt strange.

An instinct for survival

Right at the end of the Tower days I was down and quite lonely. A friend of mine, Lorri Guppy, introduced me to a chap called Neil and we hit it off straight away. I think it was because we were both in the same boat, on our own and footloose and fancy free. I stayed with Neil in his house in Barry and I loved it there. There were new people to meet and it was just a stone's throw from Cardiff. I was getting bookings in the clubs and doing okay. Then I had a chance to go to Spain. I asked Neil if he wanted to go and he said yes, so I ran upstairs to pack. We flew out to Spain and when we got there we found out that the job the agent had promised me was non-existent. I had been conned yet again! What was I going to do? It was a case of switching to Plan B. Well, I didn't really have a Plan B, just an instinct for survival.

I offered the hotel's resident pianist a night off (on me!) then I pulled out every stop. I did so well that to my amazement the management offered me their other place across the road. My God, I was saved. And so I settled down to Spanish living again, and that was *so* easy; standing in the sun all day and being adored by people at night.

After we had been there for two years we decided to go home for a while. A friend of mine told me that there was a new radio station opening up in Cardiff and that I should try for a show on it. So, home I trundled. I auditioned and got the job, and ended up loving the radio so much that I didn't want to go back to Spain. I had found my new lifeline.

Neil and I fell apart on our return. He seemed to me to be constantly unhappy and so we went our separate ways. Sad, but there you go.

Years later I was strolling along a street in Penarth and this beautiful blonde lady called to me and asked how I was. I said, 'Do I know you?' And then I realised that my ex-boyfriend was now my ex-girlfriend! Neil was now Ella, and so happy. More recently I introduced Ella to Gabe and they hit it off big time; so much so that Gabe said to me, 'Why don't you ask Ella and her boyfriend to go with us to Benidorm for your 50th birthday weekend?' They jumped at the invitation and we had a weekend of a lifetime. That was when I met Lips and Lashes, the drag act that I brought over from Benidorm to perform at one of my charity concerts at the Swansea Grand Theatre a few years back.

CHAPTER FIVE

Always on My Travels

Bitten by the bug in Belgium

I LOVE BEING ABROAD. My favourite destinations have to
be Berlin, Jersey, Spain, Gibraltar and Holland. I remember
my first trip abroad, to Belgium. My father's brother, Uncle
Eddie, lived with his wife, Betty, and their children in a
place called Berchem, near Antwerp. I was about eight
at the time and the plan was to go to visit the Belgium
contingency. It was the day I was to fly for the first time, and
I couldn't understand why I was on the toilet so much, but
I remember my mother saying that it was the excitement.
We flew from Cardiff and the plane was an Argonaut with
propellers and a Rolls-Royce Merlin engine. We climbed
aboard and sat above the wing. It was a bit noisy but that
didn't bother me. It was all too exciting. I also recall the
flying hostess bringing food around. This was all too much.
I believe that this was the trip of all trips and the one that
started it all for me – the need to travel and be abroad.

Uncle Eddie picked us up from the airport. We consisted
of me, mother, father, and my nana. I remember sitting in
this foreign car that I'd never heard of, and it seemed to be a
long trip. We moved into their house which was so different
to ours. There was no dust anywhere and the spoons looked
like Aunty Betty bleached them every day. They had strange
food on the table as well, like salamis and Parma hams and
so on, and I was a little too frightened to try them... at first!

Eventually I did and I loved it. From then on my mother's life was unbearable, as all I wanted back home in Wales was foreign food – though I usually had to make do with fish fingers.

Uncle Eddie and Aunty Betty Belgium were 'over the top' kind to me and showered me with toys that I'd never seen before and had only dreamed of. I remember a radio-controlled lorry dumper (with a wire, really) which I insisted was so special that nobody could match me in school. This is also when I discovered Cote d'Or praline chocolate. My God, I was addicted to it and so were my parents. For breakfast they put on the table chocolate vermicelli on bread and butter. This was how I wanted to live. I didn't want to go back to the Welsh way. I was hooked on the foreign touch.

The week flew and on the last day we went to visit a statue of a little boy peeing into a pool, Manneken Pis. I even had a key ring of this little boy. All the girls in school wanted to see his private parts, and two boys did as well. I have learned that there are similar statues all over Belgium, that they dress them in different costumes depending on the occasion, and that there are disputes between the various towns and villages as to which is the oldest.

I hit it off big time with my cousins Nicole, Monique, Vivienne and Peter. I remember playing a record called 'Non Ho L'Età' by Gigliola Cinquetti and falling in love with it. From time to time I play it on Radio Wales. It won the Eurovision Song Contest in 1964. I used to stare at the stars at night through my bedroom window and think that the people in Belgium were staring at the same sky as me. Boy, was I smitten with 'abroad'. Sometimes I think I shouldn't have gone, but there you go. It happened and I can't go back. I still dream of moving abroad, and that will never change, but I keep clutching straws that Wales will have its day, with cheaper prices, better weather, more liberal people, and more waiters to serve you coffee. You must think I'm on drugs with that tall order. Will it ever happen? Maybe, when I give birth to my first child!

I'm so tempted to go back to Belgium for a visit, but it's been forty years since we made contact (close lot, my family) and I don't know if they'd remember me. It might be worth a try. Gabe and I have been to Belgium several times and often considered finding where they live, contacting them and going to see them. Whether that's a good idea or not, I don't know.

Dutch luck with Olga

I was in Benidorm in 1987 (if you remember that was the year the weather people missed out on reporting the hurricane in Britain) with my then friend Neil, and life was good. I had a villa in Albir and a car and I had a following in the Torremar Apartments, in the club, like nothing on earth. The Welsh would turn up in their hundreds and I was king of the castle. I got very friendly with a couple from the Netherlands – Olga, her husband Hans and their daughter Greta. We grew very close and they were staying at the Torremar for a few months. When the time came for them to go back, it was awful... tears galore. We all cried and promised that we would meet again somehow.

About a year after we returned to Wales they came over and stayed with Neil and myself for Christmas. When they arrived I could see that things were not going to be the same. The holiday mood had gone. We had to drive to Harwich to pick them up and that was a long drive back to Wales. We were stopping every couple of miles for the Dutch to be sick! It took us ten hours to get from Harwich to Cardiff. It was a nightmare.

When we got into the house, Neil's niece would not share her room with Greta and it went downhill from then on.

They didn't like any of the food we made, and when Olga did eventually eat something she said she was feeling ill and insisted that I got the doctor. The doctor came and he went to examine her and she wouldn't let him anywhere near her. She was shouting at him in Dutch and the poor bugger was frightened of her. So was I, to be honest! I let the doctor go and apologised. What else could I do? They wanted to go home as soon as possible. We tried to get them a flight as I couldn't face another ten hours in the car with the sick bags and so on. I tried so hard to book a flight – and remember, there's no internet in 1987. It was all by phone and travel agent back then. Another nightmare.

Olga then tried to book the flight from her local travel agent in Holland and she used my phone to do it. Having spent about two hours on the phone I ended up with a massive bill. Eventually they got a flight, a connection and everything and went home! I was so worn out, I was destroyed. I said, 'Never again.'

A few years after that, my new partner Gabe and I decided to go to Holland and I called Olga to tell her that we were coming over. She insisted that we stayed with her. I wasn't sure but eventually I gave in and said we'd drop by for a few days.

When we arrived we dropped our bags off in Amsterdam and only had a backpack with us when they picked us up. We were taken to a caravan site in a place called Hoo Hoo or something and were given a small caravan to stay in. It was okay, and we got on with it. We told Olga that we wanted to go shopping and so she dropped us off and said that we would have to catch a bus back. Olga gave us all the instructions how to get back and told us that food was at 6pm. Anyway, what with all the shopping, we got back late, at about 7.30 in the evening. Well, my God, she went bloody mental, and I almost cried with shock. It was like this woman was shouting at a pair of naughty little boys. I said I was sorry and went into the little caravan, looked at Gabe and just said, 'That's her bloody lot.' The following day I asked her to drop us in Amsterdam as we wanted to see the city. She wanted to spend the day with us, so I just went along with it. When we got to Amsterdam, she said, 'You stay there and I'll go and park the car.' So off she went and I looked at Gabe and said, 'Right then, city slicker, frigging run!' and we bolted into the city. We never saw her again.

Gabe and I went exploring Amsterdam and I decided to have a peep at the red-light district. I thought to myself, 'This has got to be done.' We came to a window and there was a lady of the night, naked, sitting on this posh stool. I said to Gabe, 'Go in and find out where she got that stool.'

Now, everywhere I go, I have to have a sing. I asked (ordered) Gabe to find me a karaoke bar, and so we set off in search of my musical fix. We found a bar and went in. They were playing music and the words were coming up on the screen but the artist's voice was on it as well. It wasn't so much karaoke, more of a sing-along with your favourites. Can you imaging doing a duet with, say, Madonna or Elton John? 'Well,' I thought to myself, 'what a load of old... !' (Oops. It's Catherine Tate again!) So, *moi*, ever at the ready with backing tracks on CD, MiniDisc and MP3 (which I just happened to have in my pocket), got up and showed them how to do it. I went down a storm and we didn't pay for a drink all night. I told them I was keyboard player for Bonnie Tyler at one time and the Dutch thought I was her brother. Well, the drinks were flowing, and who was I to burst their bubble?

After a nice evening educating the Dutch, we left the bar and headed back to the hotel. On the way back we walked once again past the windows of the red-light district and one of the ladies started to lick the window and rub her private parts at me. I had never seen a woman's bits before and I was so shocked that I fell over and twisted my ankle, and

Gabe had to help me limp back to the room. (That's not all that was limp, trust me.)

We stopped in the Gerstelkorrel Hotel in Dam Square and it was lush, but when we got back that night Gabe put a cold damp rag on my ankle, which was pretty bad, and we spent the rest of the time in the hotel room ordering pizza and watching *Star Trek* in Dutch, with me translating it for him. I have to admit I enjoyed the time I was laid up. Gabe took me on a trip of the canals of Amsterdam. We loved every moment of it. We saw lots of the sights, and a few dykes as well – although we never got introduced! I loved Amsterdam; it's my type of place. We set off home, wondering if I'd ever see my Dutch friends again. We haven't, so far. To this day I don't know what happened to Olga, but there you go. As they say, 'One day the bull win, one day the matador win.'

CHAPTER SIX

On with the Show and into the Garden

'Becks and Becks'

I LOOK AT MYSELF now – Chris Needs on the radio, on the TV, on the theatre stage, writing books, fundraiser and patron to so many organisations – and think, how do I handle things now? Good question! Sometimes I find it hard being 'public property'. I feel that if I did something, like sound off in front of someone, or speak out of turn, I would probably end up on the front page of the papers. And, believe you me, I've been there. I remember talking once to the press and the subject of my mother's death came up, and how ill I was, and how I had a bit of a breakdown, and the headlines were on the front of the Sunday newspapers: 'Welsh star's darkest secret.' Make no bones about it, lots of newsagents had my name on the billboards outside the shop. That I find hard, although people are forever telling me, 'It's to be expected. It's your job.' Or is it?

I find it hard being a celebrity. I can't act in front of people, I have to be myself. I honestly believe that people look at Gabe and I as the 'Posh and Becks' of Wales. (Okay, 'Becks and Becks' then). I used to hide my sexuality, as it was so scorned years ago, but now I flaunt it. I don't mean to, but nowadays it is so acceptable to be gay that I'm enjoying being sort of normal and not being made fun of.

I love the word 'poofter' and often call myself a 'poof', even when I fill in forms. I love it! I often use the poof bit on stage. When I'm in the Swansea Grand Theatre my usual opening line on stage is, 'Thank you to Swansea city council for allowing poofs in the building' and the crowd loves it. I can't help what I am, so I just get on with it and try and have a laugh along the way.

Being the 'Becks and Becks' of Wales, I wonder if Gabe would have a tattoo? I don't think so somehow. Of course I've got to be one step ahead. I've already got two tattoos. I had them done in Benidorm years ago and I love them. I would never have them removed. Now, if I was a youngster today, would I have any tattoos done? Yes, I love them.

But what am I at this moment? An entertainer? A gay icon? I really don't know! I feel sometimes that I was given a vocation to help people. I firmly believe that, and it pleases me to do it, so I'll carry on as best I can. I don't think I'll get any bigger, career-wise. I think that this is it. I've arrived. So I'll just get on with it, and hope that the Lord will spare me, healthwise, and that the BBC will still believe in me in years to come. I don't want to go anywhere else, although I have said in the past, 'I'm freelance. I can be bought.'

Me and the Garden

My relationship with my listeners is so very special, believe you me, and to be honest I don't think there's anything like it elsewhere in the world. It's unique, and it will never be repeated. Where else can you call up someone late at night and ask advice from another listener about an operation, or what time the buses run in another part of the country? I've got to know members of Chris Needs' Friendly Garden really well over the years. I even know what tablets they are on. I love it!

I'm told nearly every day that I've made a monster, but such a nice monster I hasten to add. There's power in people

and the Garden does so much good. They are the best
at praying for people that need a little help. The Garden
encourages others to go on, and we hold old-fashioned
values, as today's values get on my bloody nerves. Which
reminds me, I must get my moat cleaned. Can you believe
it? With all the problems in the world, this country has to
dominate the world headlines with an expenses scandal by
MPs. Oh to be a government official! What a fiasco. It turns
my stomach, especially when some people can't meet the
basics, let alone pay their mortgages. It really does sicken me.

Unofficially I suppose the Chris Needs Friendly Garden
is my fan club. I think the world of my members, as they
do me. In September 2010 the Garden celebrates its tenth
anniversary, and with current membership approaching
50,000 it is impossible to name everyone for their support
and loyalty in every way. If I did, I would be on my twenty-
fifth book. The hospital appeals charity shop in Cwmafan
became the base for the Garden, a meeting point. I think,
back then, it was so listeners could have a nose at me! It was
so busy at one point that I spruced the back of the shop up
and put in tables and chairs and an awning (to protect us
from the rain) and members would call in for a free tea or
coffee and enter people into the Garden for membership.
People gave donations and Madam Yeoman gave us loads
of plants and bushes to decorate it. There was one problem
and there still is: the Japanese knotweed. It's actually
growing through the air vents of the shop and we can't get
rid of it. Help! It's not helped by the heavy rains we have.
Mind you, it looked good when it was knotweed-free. We
had painted flagstones and a trellis with climbing plants,
fair play mind! All we need now is a bit of tidy weather and
a way to get rid of knotweed and we'll be back cooking on
gas. I'll get there.

One thing I can say is that I can trust my Garden
members with my life. But I have to be honest, what is

hard is trying to keep up with them all. It's impossible!
And I feel a bit guilty when I meet someone and they say, 'I
haven't heard from you in ages,' but it is so hard to do it all.
I sometimes wade through a thousand emails a week just at
the BBC.

I'm taking my work home with me more and more,
because I believe that I don't have a job but a vocation. I
can't help it. People rely on me for company, reassurance
and guidance, and I worry so much about them. It must be
horrible to lose a partner or a child. And when I speak to
an elderly lady, I often think that this could be my mother.
I'm doing more and more outside duties now than ever, like
my hospital visits. I quite often phone listeners in the day
just to make sure that they are okay, and not still depressed,
and I think they appreciate the fact that I've put down my
tools and stopped and thought of them. I'm finding more
and more that loneliness is the key to the success of my late
show. There are so many lonely people about, and it upsets
me so much. So I get on the blower and have a right good
chat and then I feel as if I've done the right thing by them.

A loyal friend

Phil Thomas has been a dedicated Garden member for
years, and during that time we have become good friends.
Phil has always been loyal to me and Gabe. I had a call one
day from his family, saying that Phil had been taken ill and
was in hospital. His condition was very serious, had been
complicated by a virus and had nearly wiped him out. They
had to induce him into a coma and then he was linked up
to various machines which were monitoring him. They told
me that Phil had been asking for me and asked if I would be
prepared to visit him, which I did while he was recovering
in the high dependency unit. I saw him on a breathing
machine and I thought a full recovery was unlikely. He

looked so poorly. To be honest, I thought that was going
to be the last time I would see him. However, slowly but
surely his condition improved, and thank the Lord, for He
didn't want Phil yet and Phil made a fantastic recovery.
Several years before this illness, Phil was on one of my telly
programmes, *The Chris Needs Experience*, and he told his
story about coming out and his panic attacks and how he
turned his life around. Phil is a wonderful Garden member
and believes in the Garden big time. The Garden was there
for him and pulled him through quite a few times. Good
luck to you, Phil, and continued good health.

The best china for tea

The late great Dilys Morris from Treorchy was a massive
character. Due to her love of travel and knowledge of other
continents I renamed her Dilys Chalmers after the TV
celebrity Judith Chalmers and awarded her the Garden
title of Foreign Correspondent. She loved the Garden show,
phoned in frequently and was never forgotten. She was a
lady of ninety years of age and she showed on air how much
she depended on the programme. Dilys, like myself, often
repeated herself and this turned out to be addictive in a
strange way. She would tell me at least a dozen times that
she was married on Christmas Day and that her birthday
was on 21 March and mine was on 12 March. Then she'd go
on to say that she was married on Christmas Day and so the
conversation went on. People in the Garden adored her for
what she was – a lovely, dear old lady who was friendly and
God fearing.

We were invited to dinner by the Dirty Dogs, two gay
lads in the Garden, and I arranged to call in and see Dilys
on the way, as it was nearby. We went into her house and
the chocolate Swiss roll was already on the plate with some
homemade Welsh cakes, sandwiches of all sorts and, of

course, the best china for the tea. While we were there, the club up the road got to hear of my visit and they took a break from what they were doing – Bingo, I think – and they queued to see Gabe and me at Dilys' house.

The street was popping in as well. I think that must have been the most visitors that Dilys had seen in a long while. We couldn't get out to go to the Dirty Dogs' house at the time we agreed. The time we spent with Dilys was amazing. It proved to me that the Garden was working and working well. We eventually got to Kevin and Clive's house and boy, did we have a meal and a half in their amazing home; all modern and chrome and glass and white leather. And the food – when those boys put on a spread, it's fit for a queen. Well, I ought to know! And that was after all the grub we had at Dilys' house too. We all miss her loads, and none of us will ever forget her. God bless you, Dilys.

Pearl 'Barley'

What a wonderful lady Mrs Pearl Johns was. She was probably my biggest fan and nobody was allowed to mention my name badly in front of her or she'd be there, ready with a spear. I always remember when the BBC2 Wales digital television channel first came out and *The Chris Needs Experience*, my first TV programme, was due on this channel. The Garden tuned in and a lot were disappointed. They had tuned into BBC2 Wales but I was not on that one. Confusing, I know, but Pearl Barley – 'Barley' because I renamed her one mad night – started to run off copies of the programme on video, and then sent them out to Garden members who had missed it. Now that's what I call a fan.

Just moments before Pearl died in hospital she was listening to me on her headphones. The nurse wanted to remove the headphones but Pearl was having none of that. She said, 'I'm listening to my Chris,' and that's how she died, listening to me. Pearl Barley, you changed my life for the better. Love you!

The rough with the smooth

I'm very lucky with BBC Wales. They let me get on with it and fair play, mind, letting an old poofter run wild for three hours a night. I insist on good music. I won't play rubbish on my programme and the music does help. It also brings back memories.

When I do a concert, I will stay until I've seen the last person leave the building and make sure that they've all had an autograph and photos, etc.

I write a lot at home, replying to letters and emails. I have sometimes hundreds to do, what with those addressed to me at the BBC and those to the charity shop, and my own personal stuff, too. Sometimes I've sent out as many as 200 letters in a week, but I have to do this, otherwise I'd worry. I spend a lot of time sending BBC birthday cards to the Garden, and I know that they get pride of place in people's homes. I'm a lucky person to be able to do what I do, and by doing my outside duties I feel as if I'm doing my job correctly. Not just pushing buttons and giving out time checks.

Unfortunately even I get nasty and crank letters at times and, as previously mentioned, I am always told I should expect them in my position. Most annoying is that most of this correspondence comes without names or addresses that I can respond to.

Here's a few of my nasty letters:

Chris Needs.
Who do you think you are? You come on our radios and promote homosexuality. You should be shot at dawn. You don't deserve a godson as you'll be leading him up the same

*poofy garden path as you. You'll have a visit before long from
social services. They will sort you out.*

*Then you speak on the radio as if you care for others. You
only do it for the money and to rob old people and give them
false hope. You brag about your boat and your sports car and
your places abroad and your queer partner and never stop
talking about your dead mother. The BBC must have shit in
their eyes and need a wake up call. Is there something wrong
with Sam's parents? How can they trust you with him? I pray
for that child every night.*

*You said in your last book that the man that abused you
should rot in hell. I must say, some Christian you are. This
goes to prove that what I am saying is correct. You are a
con merchant and always blowing your own trumpet. Good
riddance to bad rubbish is what I say.*

(Unsigned and no address.)

Here's another, and guess what? No name, no address, no
guts!

*If I was you I would shut up, not go on and on. How can
you? I cringe when I think of what you are. How can you
say about the Lord and God, it's a cover-up. He wouldn't
be pleased with you. Why do you talk so much? We do not
want you on Saturdays and Sundays. When are you going on
holidays? Mark can take over. What a different programme,
so good as he doesn't go on and on about himself. Do you
like listening to your own voice? You are selfish. All self.*

And just another nasty letter...

*You should not be let loose in the community, you filthy
queer bastard. You moan that you never had a child. Thank
God, I say. All queers should be shot and exterminated so*

that the rest of us normal people can live our lives without the fear that freaks like you could go after one of our loved ones. I will always tune in, in case I discover something. I'm watching you and I have followed you at night. You know that I do because I have flashed you from behind. I now know where you live so be careful Mr, or is it Mrs? The thought of you and another man touching each other turns my stomach. Do the right thing and piss off somewhere else and leave us good people in Wales alone. I'm ashamed to say that I live in the same neighbourhood as you. Your mother must be turning in her grave. She should have had you terminated before you showed your queer body to the world. I hate you. You are nothing but scum and I hope you die from diabetes. If I had the chance I would run you over in the car and then I could sleep at night.

Now, in a perfect world I would have the right to reply, but just what would I say? What would I really like to say? And how offensive could I be? 'Thank you for buying my number-one-selling book and listening to my award-winning radio show. Oh, by the way, due to popular demand the Garden is now broadcast six nights a week – I so enjoy the extra show on a Saturday night.' Maybe I could just suggest that they try another radio station – politely, of course. Yeah! As if! What I really can't understand is, if these people are not happy with the show, why do they tune in regularly? Nobody is forcing them to. After all, their choice is not limited in any way, and regular listeners across the world can vouch for that.

Compliance, rules and regulations

When I was first asked to take over the night show on Radio Wales, I was given carte blanche to be myself, play my style of music and get an audience. Traditionally, this show had been regarded as the dead shift. I had the opportunity to make it my own and that's exactly what I did. No restrictions were placed on me, just every trust not to be an embarrassment to either myself or to the BBC. I do not feel that I am a disappointment to the management team. The audience grew to such an extent that only a small portion of callers who rang in were able to chat on air. The show became so successful that it was recognised as often having a larger share of the Radio Wales audience at night than most of the daytime shows achieved. In addition, Chris Needs' Garden has even achieved one of the largest shares of the radio listening figures for a night time show.

It was so strange to start with when I was on stage. When it came to the end of the outside broadcast – a live broadcast of the radio show before an audience – I would say the usual thing: 'Time once again for the BBC home service, Radio Wales, to close down for another night.' And when I looked at the audience, all I could see were the front rows. They were filling up, and the tears were falling. One lady said to me, 'Chris, don't go!' I thought to myself, I've tapped into something here. There's a lot of people out there needing companionship at night. So let's do it.

At first we had a few competitions, but soon it became mainly the questions. I'd ask what the listeners thought I might have done or said next, about where I had been or about a funny or unusual experience. It was more of a guessing game, and it gave listeners the chance to learn more about me and my lifestyle. Sometimes the answers would be so outrageous or bizarre that they had to be right! Quite often the answers or suggestions would prove to be a catalyst for listeners to ring in and tell of their experiences or problems. Others would then telephone in offering support and advice. This is how the Garden worked. An on-air community was born.

Unfortunately, not long ago a number of companies

producing high profile television shows featuring competitions began using unscrupulous tactics, inviting viewers to telephone in knowing full well that their competition lines had already closed. In some cases the winner had even been chosen, but the viewers kept ringing in on premium lines with no chance of being entered into the competitions. These television companies were profiting from shares of the telephone charges. Following various investigations this practice appeared to be widespread, and not limited to television. As a result, all competitions were banned from the radio. And, as a question constitutes a competition, for the first time my programme faced a restriction. But, hell, what did I give away? A pen or a mug, or if you were lucky and saved up your Garden points, a shopping bag or umbrella. Useful goodies.

Without the questions the number of callers dropped, though fortunately the size of the audience didn't. But the format of the programme had changed, and the Garden was not happy. No amount of letters or complaints would sway the BBC to reverse their decision. When national BBC radio stations recommenced competitions, and even when some of the perpetrators did so, they still weren't brought back to Radio Wales. It's such a shame that the questions on my programme have been struck off, all over that lot in London fiddling the prizes. Hopefully they will come back as I know the Garden misses them terribly and they were the essence of the programme.

Then there was the disgusting saga with two presenters/ comedians who verbally abused a respected actor and his family in a series of telephone calls – a program that was recorded and yet transmitted without being edited. As a direct result of this I now have to have a producer present in the studio, as there are live phone calls, which is thought to be high risk. I was very uncomfortable about having a producer on my show. I do not take kindly to being told

what to do, or when and how to do it. I will start the CD
when I press the button, not when I get told to. This show
was my idea. I invented it and I didn't want someone
interfering with me performing and spoiling it. A supervisor
for Chris Needs? Never!

Interviews were done and a young cockney lad was
appointed to the job of producer. I hated even the thought
of this but was assured that no changes were to be made;
things would stay the same and this new young lad would
supervise the phone calls in case anyone said a swear word
or something.

I was gunning for him but, I have to say, he knows his
place and he's been a terrific help, too, not interfering
but doing all the shitty hard work. He is good for the
programme. More importantly, we get on very well. (Lucky
for him, as I wouldn't like to have a run in with me.) He
leaves me to it when I'm performing and is truly a good lad.
Welcome to my world, Chris Bolton. Now, imagine him if
you can. Here's a picture of Chris: he wears *gay* cardigans (I
wouldn't wear them – can't get on with knitwear!) and has a
better handbag than me (okay, it's a sort of LP/courier bag)
but doesn't belong to my tribe. He might have quite a soft
spot for Wales, and has a Welsh girlfriend, too. I try to look
after him as best as I can, like I do everybody. I make sure
he eats fruit every night, even though he prefers chocolate!
Chris B really does like my programme and respects me for
what I have achieved. I keep an eye on him and he chuckles
to himself if I do a funny. I think he's developing a Welsh
sense of humour, and a fake Welsh accent as well.

So far, things are okay, but in this very unsure world we
have to keep our fingers crossed that there's not another
national fiasco that is going to affect us here in Wales. The
producer role suits me fine at the moment, but I would
like to see the return of the questions as soon as possible.
Everyday when I am out and about I am stopped and asked,

'When are those questions coming back, Chris Needs?'

One of my favourites on the phones has to be Kirsty (as well as Gabe, of course). She came on board about five or six years ago. I didn't think she'd like it, but how wrong I was! First of all she is a mega fan of the music and she loves the contact with the listeners. Her dad is Alistair, who used to be my producer; the man with the shorts and big appetite. I leave everything to Kirsty, as I do Gabe, and I never have to question anything. She just gets on with it in her own wonderful way. She supports me big time; she will not let me walk to my car on my own and puts everything away at the end of the night. I nip for a pee and by the time I've arrived back she's done the computers, headphones, CDs... the lot!

Kirsty only filled in to start with but boy, oh boy, are we pleased she stayed on. The phone answerer has always been involved in my programme; that's the way I like it. They are the first port of call to the programme so it's important to have the right person on board. Sometimes people just phone up and ask to leave a message for me, but I think they really want a little chat with someone, and she's the girl to put things right. Very often when I've nipped into her room to make a cuppa, I've listened to her talking to people and giving them good advice. She is a treasure. Kirsty used to do two nights a week with me, but with other commitments she has had to cut it down to one.

Since the BBC have stopped me asking questions, I have to try and fill the programme with something else, and the album of the week is proving to be a hit. I was given a CD to play which had several different local Welsh singers on it. I played everyone on the album, but then a little while after I was sent a very insulting email saying that I didn't play one of the artistes. Now let's face it, I don't have to play any of them but I do because it promotes Welsh talent.

The email was very insulting to me, saying that he was

never going to listen to me again and so on. The funny thing was that I *did* play her *and* on the first night. The emailer portrayed himself as being a fan of this girl and when my senior producer wrote back stating that I had played her, he wrote back again asking if we were listening to the same radio station as him. Quite insulting, again. I smelt a rat (I'm good at that) and I found out that it was this girl's father pretending to be a fan. When he was rumbled, he sent in another email saying he was sorry. Does he not realise that I was only trying to promote his daughter? It was very hurtful, but then I've seen this a million times over; the pushy parent. All they do is ruin their children's chances of getting on.

Chris Needs Talent

I'm called a grumpy old bugger by lots of people, especially Gabe, but I am not. What I'm doing is stating a fact about something that is not satisfactory. Great Britain, in my mind, is done for. It's the dumping ground of Europe. It has no identity and the rest of the world pisses themselves laughing at it. I don't want to be known as British, in fact I'm the furthest away from being a Brit.

I am totally embarrassed about the way some young people act, and about older people who drink too much. I don't like the insular attitude, as if the world starts at Fishguard and ends at Chepstow. I have to be completely honest, when I used to go back to Cwmafan I'd feel an air of disapproval, as if some people didn't want to see me get on.

Cardiff people seemed to be more *for* me than anyone else anywhere. They have everything in Cardiff, and to see celebs walking down the street with chips in paper is nothing. They are not fazed one bit. I had come to terms with how things were and just got on with it and ignored the crap. But then things changed, dramatically...

Recently I was looking forward to, and at the same time dreading, performing at Dylan's in Cwmafan. The last time I went there I died on my backside. I asked Maria Lyn to be my support and she did a good job, as usual, warming up the people ready for me. It was time to go on to do my spot and, as you may know, I like to do my comedy. Not dirty, but shop soiled. So I walked on stage to 'Everything's Coming Up Roses'. It felt good. The room was full and I could see that many of the people there enjoying themselves had been in infants' school with me. After the song, the response was good and I battled with the comedy, always giving a ribbing to Roy Noble. The night turned out to be stonking and I've been asked to return. While I was in deep negotiations with the owner, Gareth Brennan, we came up with the idea of a talent show. This is something I have always wanted to do, a 'Chris Needs Talent' show. I'm glad my name came in handy for something. (Move over Simon Cowell!)

Even though I hate the name Needs, because of the ridicule I suffered in school, in this instance it would work well. This show could give a lot of openings to young local artistes looking for experience on stage and would possibly lead on to a profession. I would like to host the talent show annually. My mother was a suppressed artiste (and don't I know it) and if she had had the chance to have that mentoring, I think she would have really been someone in the limelight. So, this talent show means a lot to me and I shall endeavour to look for new Welsh talent as long as I can.

I actually heard Gareth Brennan, the owner, singing live and I loved his voice. It was so high; not like me, down in my boots. I loved being back in Cwmafan and it brought lots of memories back to me. Sheridan Davies was there. She was in school with me and she gave me a photograph of me and her sitting on her father Glan's car. The hair was still a mess. Mine I mean.

Chris posing again (second right) at Cwmafan Infants School

Chris and his mother, Margaret Rose at her all time favourite place – 'Rhododendron Drive' on Jersey. She loved these flowers.

Dad, Aitch with one of his many gardening awards ... what blooms are they?

Chris and his mum, together with her cousins

Lady Kathryn and Countess Christine

Chris' mother, Margaret
Rose. Her two great loves;
that for her Lord and
being in Jersey

Gabe and Chris in Corfu

Posing in Ibiza

Climbing back on board, Corfu

Island hopping in Greece

With 'Mam' Elsie
Hepplewhite, actress
Margaret John

Bruce Anderson duets with
Mandy Starr

Ben Howells performs
with mum, Maria Lyn at St
David's Hall

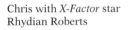

Chris with *X-Factor* star
Rhydian Roberts

Chris and his special guest
Max Boyce at the Variety
Club awards ceremony

Chris receives a Lifetime Achievement Award from the Variety Club of Great Britain

Hosting the annual Beaufort Male Choir charitable fundraiser

Chris and the June Bois Dancers

Duet with Gillian Elisa: 'Baby it's cold outside'

Chris and friends celebrate his 40 Years in Showbusiness at St David's Hall

Pulling faces; Chris, Sammy and Lightning McQueen

Sammy learning to read with Chris

Sammy following in his Dad's footsteps, on stage at St David's Hall

Checking out Dad's new spectacles

A perfect gentleman at Chris' award ceremony

Chris at the heart of the Garden, the BBC studios at Broadcasting House, Cardiff

Chris equally at home with his baby grand as he is in the studio

Maria Lyn recording a duet with Chris

Chris having fun with his audience

Cast photo of the Swansea Grand Theatre show

Chris and dancing partner; Hawaiian Bar, Jersey

Again at the Hawaiian Bar, Jersey, a mere kid

With entertainer David Copperfield, again in Jersey ... the first is David using Chris as a ventriloquist's dummy ...

Mother and son, Jan Ross duets with Bruce Anderson

Carol Llewellyn of the Variety Club with Bruce and Jan Ross

David Emanuel in concert at Chris' 40th extravaganza

Chris with straight hair

Action! The official launch of the Swansea Bay International Film Festival 2009

Chris, preparing the garden at the rear of the charity shops

Chris in reflective mood at home

Christmas must be approaching, Benidorm, Spain

Holly Holyoake, Maria Lyn, Bruce Anderson and Ben Howells at the Variety Club award for Chris

The June Bois Dancers

French bread rolls

Chris with Bonnie Tyler

Ella

Diane Cousins

Bruce, Ben Howells, Maria Lyn and David
Emanuel, backstage at St David's Hall

Portland Mayor, Sam Adams with Chris viewing the craft work displays at the West Coast Americymru Eisteddfod, 2009

Chris with Garden members Bill Watkins and his wife SunHui from Washington State

Gabe, jet lagged and dazzled in Times Square

Chris at Trump Towers

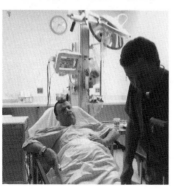

Gabe, always with a book to hand. BBC outside broadcast at Pwllheli

Chris taking a break; nothing more serious than an asthma attack: Portland Hospital

Kim Jukes and mum Shirley Stubbs

BBC producer Chris Bolton

Chris signing autographs at the Pembrokeshire show. Another BBC outside broadcast

Kirsty

Gwenda and Geinor

Media Mogul, Binda Singh

With Claire Summers at Chris' Lifetime
Achievement Award

Sarah Barry-Williams

Maria Lyn and Gabe

Wendy Cane ... my fairy Godmother

Rebecca Evans

The ever reliable Lenny Dee

Chris meeting with Mae Foy on the steps of St Patrick's Cathedral, New York

Chris with the girls, Christine, Jan and Audrey.

Polly Perkins and Chris

Polly Perkins and Teddi Munro

Well, you know me: always making plans. I just can't sit still waiting for the phone to ring. I am really looking forward to hosting the talent show and perhaps nurturing a few of the future big Welsh stars. But whatever I do, it's always got to be bigger and better than what I've already done. There's this book (the second part of my autobiography), the Jenkins's's's's's cartoon winning the Swansea Bay Film Festival animated section (where's that going to lead to then?), my first book reaching number one and being followed by *The Jenkins's's's's's' Diaries*, my lifetime achievement award from the Variety Club, the MBE and the invitation to perform in America. Also, I've been invited onto a national television programme to be interviewed about the high listening figures of the Garden show. Oh yes, and my single 'You've Got A Friend' was the bestselling CD in Wales. I am so proud that this CD has done so well and that Diabetes in Wales research benefited from all the proceeds.

Then there are meetings set up for me to have my own telly show, and my stage work in theatres and traipsing out and about is getting more popular. But whatever people say to me, I don't have that much confidence in myself usually, so let's see what happens. Telly would be nice, but not at the expense of the radio.

There are two places where I position myself behind a microphone – on the radio and on stage. They are very different, I must admit, and this concert in Cwmafan has done me so much good. I now feel as if people, my people, really do enjoy what I do and that is very important to me. I'm glad to say that now everything connects, and the books and the stage shows, the CDs and the radio are all as important as each other. Long may it continue.

CHAPTER SEVEN

Variety is the Spice of Life

The Garden gathering

'THE BIG SHOW' AS I call it, is the variety show called 'Chris Needs And Friends'. It has turned into a Garden gathering and fundraiser, a meeting place for all of us. But I think the variety show is an opening for young and new artistes.

Bruce Anderson, Mandy Starr and Holly Holyoake have been some of the success stories, and I have to say there are more and more new artistes walking on my stage and I love it. I wish I'd had the chance to perform on a theatre stage when I was a lad. I had to put up with clubs.

The show is always filmed and a copy is sent to each of the artistes as a personal thank you. Then they can put it on their website or on YouTube so the world can see them in a wonderful environment, not in a backstreet pub with drunks all around. This really does work and I get numerous requests to put people on the show, just to do one number, which I do whenever I can. Can you imagine sending off a video of yourself singing at St David's Hall with dancers and lighting and so on? It's so good. The variety show raises money for diabetes and a few other causes, but I'm thrilled that it also promotes new talent.

I love putting together variety shows. Variety is the spice of life! I was chatting one day to Teddi Munro and we were reminiscing about the first time we met, which was at a variety show on HTV called *Showcase*. I just happened to say that I'd love to do that sort of thing again as the two of us were brought up in variety, and we decided to put on a show.

The first one was at the Porthcawl Grand Pavilion. I didn't know how to book a theatre. So I phoned and had a chat to the management and the next thing I knew I had booked the main hall at Porthcawl. I had never done this sort of thing before and I began to worry. What if people didn't turn up? How was I going to get them in? I had to do something for charity and this was the way forward.

People in the Garden spread the word. Mark Drane still is my handsome boy! If he believes in the event he's a one-stop shop publicity machine. And then came the task of choosing the artistes to go on the show. One of the first to be booked was Mandy Starr. As you know, she's a mighty fine singer and the Garden love her. Mandy has done most of the shows and remains a firm favourite. Then Bruce Anderson came along. His first time on my show was at Swansea Grand Theatre. He really was the new boy on the block at the Grand, but he's returned there many times since. The last Garden Variety Show at the Swansea Grand was like Bruce in concert.

Cornered by the cheese counter in Tesco's Penarth

I always try to offer the best of entertainment by using a good mix of acts, i.e. complete variety. One year we had a drag act on stage and they worked well. The show needs a bit of classical, a bit of opera, lots of jokes, dancing, a top of the bill – which people say is me – but I like to call in a big name and give the people a real big treat. Someone like Rebecca Evans, who I cornered by the cheese counter in Tesco's Penarth. How could she refuse me? Well, for a star with such an impressive and international following I was surprised, and so proud, that she confirmed the date straight away. She jumped at the chance of being on my show. My God, after all the places she's sung. It makes me wonder sometimes.

What can I say? I was speechless. I did manage to thank her and give her a tub of seriously strong cheese, and in return she bought me a lottery ticket. The cheese was a big hit – her family are now addicted to it – but the lottery ticket went down the Swanee! Rebecca was top of the bill, but who was going to play for her? So I asked – well, begged – Jeffrey Howard from Cardiff who works with Only Men Aloud and he stepped in to play for Rebecca when he really should have been in London and, yet again, for nothing. Those two are so wonderful: talented, professional and generous of their own time. They restore it all for me! These simple acts mean so much to me, especially when so many can benefit.

On the bill

There has to be good continuity in a variety show, and Teddi and I are left holding that baby. It's also a nice feeling to expose new artistes, like Maria Lyn and her son, Ben Howells. Their first booking with me was at St David's Hall. Talk about starting at the top of the tree. Since then Maria has supported my touring shows on a regular basis and it works very well.

Let's take a look at some of the other acts that have been on Chris Needs And Friends. You might remember Phillip Arran, aka CC Swan. Such a good singer and a clever drag act, too. He's now doing well in the West End in *Priscilla, Queen of the Desert*, the stage show musical. And about time as well. On the summer scorcher tour, a BBC tour of Welsh towns, we had Connie Fisher performing on my show at the Torch Theatre. Little did we know what would happen to her. Now that's the thing: a star can emerge at any time, just overnight. We are all so pleased for Connie. She was an absolute delight to work with.

Once we had a Swansea male vocalist on the show and I told him to address the people as 'the Garden'. He looked at me a bit dull and went on to say, 'Good evening, ladies and gentlemen,' and the audience looked at him daft. They were used to being addressed as 'the Garden'. He soon came around to our way of thinking.

While I was compiling Swansea Grand Theatre 2009, I was chatting to Eve Sherratt, the Swansea opera singer. She was telling me that she would have loved to have done a number or two, but she was flying off to Athens to sing that evening. Just then she had a call saying that she wasn't going until the next day. 'Count me in,' she said, then walked on and did 'An Unexpected Song'. She sang just the one song and brought the house down.

I try to make the show resemble the Royal Variety Show. Patricia O'Neill always turns out a tidy singer with her coaching, and there's a few to come yet from her talent shows. Patricia has to be one of my biggest fans ever. I have also been fortunate enough to have worked with her. Pat runs a wonderful show called 'Can You Sing?' which discovers new talent here in Wales and I've been a part of this show. There is now a Chris Needs Award associated with the show. The youngsters are so good that I've got an unlimited stream of up and coming artistes for my variety shows. One of Pat's lads was Arwel Thomas. He did tremendously well on one show. I reckon he has a bright future in front of him. I'm still looking for a plate spinner or a knife thrower. God help health and safety! Pat seems to me to be the Simon Cowell of Wales, and probably has as many connections in the business. You might remember the names Andrew and Dennis O'Neill? Keep going, Pat!

One piece of advice. And, believe me, this is so true. The golden rule is: be sweet to people on the way up, as you might need them on the way down.

On with the show

The opening is so important to a show. I like to have a fanfare and always do. For my '40 Years In Entertainment' I hired in a big silver screen for the St David's Hall show in Cardiff and had a collage of gay artistes throughout the years. I had Dorothy Squires singing 'I Am What I Am' over a slideshow featuring the likes of Freddie Mercury, Dusty Springfield, Pat Clements (Pat Butcher), Elton John, Johnny Mathis and the list went on. Being the cheeky bugger that I am, I wanted to put some government ministers in the middle but Gabe persuaded me not to, telling me to be professional. My answer, as usual, was, 'Balls to that!' At the end of the collage there was a picture of me, and then I walked out in front of the audience to a wonderful round of applause. (Okay, so I got the idea from Katherine Jenkins' show 'Viva La Diva'. She had a similar opening, though not quite as queer as mine.)

My opening line at St David's Hall was, 'Thank you to Cardiff City Council for letting poofs in legally.' Yep, it seems to fit nicely wherever I am performing. I had a standing ovation for that alone, and that was before I'd started. Then once the crowd had quietened down, I said, 'You'll never guess why I've called this meeting tonight.' More laughter. I went on to say that it was exactly 40 years to the very week that I had started in the business, and that I'd enjoyed it so much I'd decided to do another forty years. More applause.

I'm getting a bit like Ken Dodd. You can't get me off the stage. I seem to cling to the fact that I'm in my favourite place: in front of an audience, be it on stage or on air. The amount of times I have said I would love an office job, and that it would be nice to have sick money and holiday money... but I think if I had to tick boxes and count tins on a shelf for a living I would be in the cuckoo house. Trust me! If I had to put on a collar and tie and say, 'Good morning, you're through to Fred Bloggs & Partners; Chris speaking; how may I help you?' I would end up saying something in Russian – that is, something ending in 'off'. (Oh, Catherine Tate's nana springs to mind once again!)

The June Bois Dancers have been forever faithful and still are today. I remember Teddi suggesting them and we gave them a whirl. They grew and grew as time went on, showing great interest, and always turned up with new outfits and routines. The shows have given them a chance to bloom, and in return they have given us performances with that bit of finesse that we so desperately needed. Long may they continue. There are three generations working within the school: June, the grandmother; Michelle, the daughter; and Tammy, the granddaughter. Then there are all the girls and the costume makers – a really professional troupe. I never forget the first time I sang on stage and had dancers all around me. I felt like a star. Lots of the girls have moved on to be top professionals, dancing on summer seasons, and doing the cruises, etc. Nice one!

I have to keep the show fresh, which means leaving out (in the nicest possible way) some of the regulars. It's hard juggling them around because they do their own thing as well, and sometimes they are already booked. I usually end up with three on one show and thirty-three on another. So devising the show is such a crucial part, and a hard part as well, as I don't want to upset anybody. Being in the theatre is very special to me, and to the other artistes also. It's not every day that we can be in a theatre environment, as there's not enough stage work to be had, especially with the recession and that damn credit crunch. People are faced with decisions like, 'Do I buy groceries or pay the electricity or do I buy a ticket for a show?' It's damn hard at the moment.

To be honest I'm surprised that things are still going, and hearing the news doesn't always help. We never seem to take the lead in anything positive; even trailing when other countries in Europe are coming out of the recession. I wonder where our funds, our taxes are going. We seem to be engaged in other people's wars and it costs so much money, yet we constantly hear that our troops are under-funded and that they don't have the right equipment. So why are they sent away? If we cannot support them, the money being spent (wasted?) could be better spent on health, say, rather than contributing to the loss of our soldiers' lives. Boy, would I like to be in power.

I love Porthcawl Pavilion. It has its own special charm. The show there turns out to be a Garden Party; that's when the friendly Garden comes out in force. Swansea Grand seems to be a prestige type of place. It has a history for me. I can always remember being there with my mother watching Ryan and Ronnie, and my mother would tell me, 'Study that man Ryan. He's a good role model. Trust in your mother!'

Keep your children children

Now then, I did pantomime with Stan Stennett once. Stan had asked me for years to be in his panto and I never had the time because of the late show. It does tend to restrict my options for evening work outside the BBC. But Stan assured me that I could be away from the panto in time to comfortably get to the studio and do my programme, so I started the tour.

I played Sunny the Gardener, who was a bit 'twp' and gay. God help us! It went fine in the beginning, but I think it took its toll on me, sometimes doing three shows a day, which was in addition to my radio show at night. My health started to play up. So much, in fact, that I immediately stopped smoking. To be honest I was a little frightened to continue smoking. My goodness, something was up. However, it was a very interesting run and I learned a lot from Stan.

I always remember Stan saying on stage at the end of the show, 'It's nice to see the children excited and enjoying the panto. Mums and dads, keep your children children for as long as you can.' I was amazed at Stan's stamina. A truly amazing guy and a good friend to me.

I'm still trying my best to put on shows and it's getting harder by the day. I won't give up as I believe people need a good laugh, especially today in this crazy world we live in. By the way, thank you for all your support in attending the shows.

Lifetime award

In 2008 the Variety Club of Great Britain contacted me and mentioned that they wanted to honour me with a 'Lifetime Achievement' award. On hearing this I thought my life was over. No, I was really thrilled.

Caryl Llewellyn was the lady who contacted me in the beginning and it was such a buzz. Being honoured by my peers! The luncheon was at the Mercure Holland House Hotel in Cardiff. People were invited to buy a table at £30 per head and there would be around 10 people to a table. There must have been about 300 plus attending.

There was a master of ceremonies with the red coat and a hammer, and there was an array of Garden members and celebrities to support not only me but this afternoon of fundraising on behalf of the Variety Club. As you know, the organisation supplies minibuses and coaches for use by disabled and disadvantaged children, to enhance their outlook and quality of life. I have been honoured to present one of the Sunshine coaches to a school in Swansea. I am so proud to be a part of the Variety Club of Great Britain.

We opened the luncheon with some sterling music – 'The Soldier's Dream' by Josef Locke. Everyone waved their hankies in the air, it was camp as hell. There were raffles and quizzes, Irish bingo and auctions, and competitions galore.

I had a top table. On my left sat Sammy and on my right sat Gabe. What more could I ask for? Well, there were a few more. There was Li Harding, the jazz singer and chef from Aberystwyth, Gabe's family, and Bruce's too, Christine from Durham flew down and Ginge from Bath was there. Of course there were Countess Christine and Lady Katherine, Roger Cwmdare, Carol and Megan, Cynthia Bolton travelled down from Rhyl, still recovering from an ankle injury, and Margaret Rich from the Heath in Cardiff came on her first trip out for ages. Oh, how she enjoyed and loved to talk about 'her' special day on the radio.

The Variety Club asked who I wanted to pay tribute to me and I had only one person in my mind: Max Boyce. I am so glad that he agreed to do it. It made my day. When he started his speech about me, he pretended not to know me and referred to me as Shane Ritchie. Max came out with some belters and made people who didn't normally smile laugh their heads off. He talked about me having north Walian fans and spoke of being a star in your own village. He said that when you go to Pontrhydyfen there's a sign that says: 'Pontrhydyfen, the birthplace of Richard Burton, Ivor Emmanuel and Rebecca Evans.' Then, he added, you go around the corner into Cwmafan and it says on the sign: 'Cwmafan/Cwmavon. Please drive carefully.' Says it all, really, doesn't it?

I was given the award – a stunning glass star on top of a comet trail – by the Variety Club's Peggy Doidge and I was totally in tears. Sam sat there for several hours and loved every moment of it. He had a chicken dinner, a meal fit for a man *and* had extra carrots. He was given fivers from two Garden members and then went on to tell me, 'Two ladies give me these fivers for Tenerife.' He enjoys his holidays; must take after his godfather!

The day included fine singers and very dear friends: Mandy Starr, Bruce Anderson, Maria Lyn and her son Ben Howells and Holly Holyoake. When the day was over I went home tired but feeling a million dollars (better than the Euro!). My mantelpiece gets smaller everyday.

CHAPTER EIGHT

Television and More...

Very Annie Mary

GABE AND I WERE on holiday for two weeks in Gibraltar when I had a call from a lady called Sara Sugarman. She wanted me to fly to London to audition/read for a part in the film that became *Very Annie Mary*. She kept on and on and on, and in the end I gave in.

Gabe drove me to Malaga airport and I flew to London, where I was picked up and taken to a hotel. The following day I went to the audition/read-through session. Philip Madoc was there, as was Mary Hopkin, and a load of Welsh stars. It was an honour to be in their company. I read my part and I was told that I was wonderful. However, I missed 'Gib' terribly, and wanted to go back there and then. The compliments were flying, but I lost four days of my holiday. When it came to the casting of the film I was dropped like a ton of bricks. Well, it felt like that anyway. I felt very bitter towards a lot of the film people and it took a bit of time to get over the knock. I was more upset that I had given up my precious time in Gib. Another lesson learned.

High Hopes

I was approached by the BBC Wales drama people – well, Boyd Clack to be honest – to appear in the comedy series *High Hopes*. Boyd asked if I fancied doing the part of the lost twin. I said that I would love to do it, and he set about writing the part. It was written especially for me as a radio presenter, and resembled the show that I already did. They called me Chris Desire, and I had this amazing conversation with 'Mam' Elsie Hepplewhite, played by Margaret John. I was the baby she gave away. The part was enormous and it was a big thing for me to do. It was such a raving success that I couldn't walk down the road without someone calling me Elvis – which is what 'Mam' had called me at birth.

I made new friends by doing that programme, and Margaret John has since appeared at the Grand in Swansea in my Chris Needs And Friends show. I stood on the stage and started to have a bit of a go at 'Mam' for calling me Elvis and saying that I was her twin son that she'd given away at birth. And while I was having a right good go at her, she walked out onto the stage with her pinafore on and said, 'Elvis, come to Mam.' The audience went off their heads, screaming, etc, and I ran to her saying, 'Mam, I've been bad.' The crowd went crazy, but all of this was in the name of a good cause: charity.

Boyd Clack and I have been talking about future projects together, including a radio play. Watch this space. I am always up for a challenge!

I hope they repeat my episode again. You get nice repeat fees doing telly. I was a bit worried at doing this part, but I have to admit 'Mam' Margaret was there holding a flag for me, and she made sure I did the right thing. It's okay if you are doing parts day in day out, but as for me it's once in a blue moon.

In the evening, when *High Hopes* was just about to be recorded in front of a live audience, a young chap from Cwmafan called Lee came up to Broadcasting House in Cardiff to see the recording of the programme. He was such a big fan, and I asked the cast to pop into my dressing room to meet him. I believe he's still talking about it today. I hope there's a new series to come. My character wasn't written out so a guest appearance wouldn't be out of the question.

Pobol y Cwm

I had planned a holiday in January one particular year. Gabe and I were going to Spain. Then the Welsh language soap *Pobol y Cwm* called me and offered me the part of Terry Donovan the psychic. I, of course, said a massive yes and the script was sent to me. It was again a big part and it frightened me. Gabe was more used to scripts and broke it down into sections, but he's not a Welsh speaker so I had to call in the troops, i.e. Gillian Elisa from the soap. She does the acting bit all the time, unlike me. She managed to get me there in one piece and it went well. Cheers, Gill.

In that episode I had to act opposite Donna Edwards, who played Britt in the series. She got drunk in the pub and was all over me and had to be shipped out – another great lady of Wales. Donna and I met while the both of us were working on a film called *Angry Earth*. Now here's another Welsh actress that always holds a flag for me. We hit it off straight away and became great friends.

It was strange in those days as she was an established actor, being the leading lady in several programmes such as *Dinas, Belonging, Tair Chwaer* and *Off to Philadelphia in the Morning*. She's been in so many things. And when we went out together for a meal, or what have you, she would always be recognised and I would be just sitting there next to her. She pushed for me to get on, and introduced me to lots of people, but success only came when Touch AM Radio happened in 1990. Then there was the Sony Radio Awards and the rest is history, as they say. I never thought radio would be my forte as I always thought piano would be the thing. But there you go. I can now do both... and I'm having a ball.

Binda le Bhaji

One of my best friends ever is Binda Singh. We met when
I was a baby on Touch Radio and we certainly became a
right click. We used to be called 'the Kray Twins'. Binda is a
Sikh but was brought up in Swansea. He speaks Welsh and
Punjabi and sometimes wears a turban with a Welsh dragon
on the front of it. He has helped me through my career like
nobody else on earth. And without even trying, we are like
brothers. He leaves me out of nothing, and has saved my
skin so many times. He is completely honest with me and
tells me things that only a true friend would.

Binda is doing so well at the moment with film festivals
all around the world, and keeps asking me to go with him,
but with time and all that nonsense, it's a bit difficult to
just nip off. Binda used to be on the late-night phone-in
on Touch Radio in Cardiff and I was on after him on the
overnight show, *Two-til-Six*. That's where I learned my trade.
I always took food in for Binda, and one particular evening I
took cheese and onion sandwiches into the studio. He loved
them and he had a sandwich in one hand and a mug of tea
in the other. Then it happened... he dunked his cheese and
onion sandwich in the tea. I felt sick. Then he went on to
say that the best was yet to come. That was drinking the tea
with the onions floating on the top!

We are still thick as thieves, and love putting on shows
here, there and everywhere. He is one of the most clever
men I have ever met in my life and when it comes to the
media he is a god. There's nothing he doesn't know. It's good
to have a friend like Binda. I feel as if I have a big brother to
look after me, and look out for me.

Camp am Ganu

Talking of music and shows, I remember the telly
programme called *Camp am Ganu* (*Singing Game*). Dafydd
Du was the question master and I was the camp one on
the piano. I wonder if this play on words would have been
accepted years ago? I doubt it. It was a musical quiz show
in Welsh and it had been planned for a while. When the
time came to do it, it was a fortnight after my mother had
suddenly died. I was a total mess and didn't know if I could
do the show. As I remember, I was constantly breaking down
and going into depression. I did it but it nearly killed me.

The BBC's senior producer of entertainment at that time
was Geraint Evans, a lovable man who helped me through
this very bad time. I managed to get through the eight TV
shows and by the end of it I didn't want to see a TV studio
ever again in my life. It was not long after that that my stint
on Radio Cymru came to an end. I thought the end of the
world had come, but it was a blessing in disguise as this was
the start of the birth of the Garden. After all, I couldn't be on
two stations at the same time.

I often wonder if the Garden would work in Welsh. I
think so, as a lot of my listeners are Radio Cymru people
and they switch over in the night to Radio Wales. The 'gogs'
(north Walians) and Welsh speakers I think accept me
working in English as they know that I am a very proud
Welsh speaker, even though I'm not proud of the weather.
It's such an embarrassment. Anyway the *Camp am Ganu*
show went out. I wasn't that fussed on it, I think because it
was so close to the death of my mother.

Turning the other cheek

I went to a club to do a charity show in the Swansea valley
and I met the compere for the evening, with his stinking
shirt and white socks and sandals. Maria Lyn and I were

on the show together and I could see it coming: I was encroaching on this man's territory. When Maria finishes she introduces me, or her last song is a duet, and when we've finished the duet she walks off and I stay on. We've always done that. Well, at the end of the night this compere went mental. He talked all the way through my last song and when I came off he had a right good go at me, saying things like 'You are a pile of crap' and 'You'll never come back here again'. Pissed talk. He then said to me, 'What do you f***ing know about putting on a show? I could do your radio show standing on my head.' I said back to him, 'I could give you a bit of advice. Try wearing a suit and having a f***ing wash, you dirty bastard.' You can tell that I wasn't in chapel at that precise moment. He had to be told. He threw the money at me and I picked it up from the floor. Do you know, I hate men. I love women but *'men'* men – well this one, anyway – they're a real pain in the arse. I think the word I'm looking for is 'Neanderthal'.

I remember once bumping into a supposed friend who was at the toilet at a function along with other celebs. When I walked in he was peeing in one of the troughs and I immediately made for the cubicle. Full of bravado, this git said, 'Backs against the wall, lads. Needsie's here.' So I said back, 'You lot are as safe as houses. It's only men I'm after.' Boy, did he look a dickhead, and rightly so. I have to admit that I'm fed up of turning the other cheek.

I did a charity show in a working men's club in Gwent and, I have to be honest, I'm frightened of nothing. I did my bit and went into the men's room at the back with my handbag. (Okay, man bag!) This fat guy, drunk and full of tattoos, came up to me and said, 'Are you Chris Needs?' I said, 'Yes.' Then he went on to say, 'What you do for lonely people, sick people and people who have lost a partner is truly incredible.' He then offered his hand to shake mine. I said as loud as I could, 'You're about to shake the hand of a homosexual.' He said, 'I don't give a f**k what you are. Put it there, butt!' Have I broken down barriers or what?

I find it hard doing shows outside Wales. Wales for me is like Hollywood. I do quite well in Benidorm, but if I go somewhere in England I become next week's act, so I tend to stick to my territory. I'm often asked to do a show in Bristol. Mmmm, now that might work. There's lot of listeners in the West Country and maybe one day I'll play a small venue. Lady Lyn, one of our dedicated Garden members from Bristol, can be the compere!

Other ambitions

Well, for starters, I want sing live with Steve Balsamo and The Storys. I hope he reads this and takes the hint. Always remember, there's many a good tune played on an old fiddle. And you know what they say about a creaking gate...

I start to plan shows for the future and, to be honest, sometimes it's a bit of a bad thing to do. I usually end up planning and scheming all night. Gabe gets up for work and I'm still going for it like a good one. Gabe is half asleep and I'm rehearsing a new routine on the kitchen floor with my tap shoes on.

Do I want to do TV?

People are forever saying to me, 'You ought to have your own TV show,' and to be honest, I think now would be a good time for me to do one. As long as it's not at the expense of the radio.

I'm thinking of a chat show, possibly called *My Pink Sofa* which would be very gay-orientated, with guests, of course, and me playing the grand piano out of tune for them just like Les Dawson did. I think it could be a cross between Cilla's *Surprise Surprise* and a whacky chat show, chopsing away to celebrities. I'd like to have Katherine Jenkins on. Do you think she could sing along to my bum notes? Another guest I'd like would be Victor Spinetti – but who would be interviewing who? We've both got more chops than a butcher's shop. Then, Margaret John, of course; Bonnie Tyler to catch up on all the gossip; Catherine Zeta-Jones, Rebecca Evans, Dame Shirley and Gwyn Hughes Jones the tenor. Let's face it, after all the years of being called a queen by my own countrymen, I think it's about time that I sat on a throne chatting with my loyal subjects, don't you?

I remember watching HTV Wales for years when the channel used continuity people announcing the programmes like Dilwyn Young Jones, Margaret Pritchard, Jenny Ogwen and Arfon Haines Davies. I used to really admire them. I recall not long ago walking out of the canteen in the BBC and Arfon was walking in. I just smiled and he said, 'Hello, Chris.' I thought, 'My God, he knows who I am!' I felt as if I had made it. I know it sounds daft, but that's me.

The best thing about being on the morning show was that I got to speak to different celebrities. I remember interviewing Honor Blackman and she said to me at the end of the interview, 'I like you.' I walked around the BBC feeling like John Steed off *The Avengers*. Then there was Margarita Pracatan, the Cuban singer. She was wild. I asked her if she was having a fling with Clive James, who had introduced her to the British public on his television show, and she answered me by saying, 'You should always listen to your mama and your God and have no Bongo Bongo.' I saw the Welsh singer Mary Hopkin walking down a corridor once, just a few years back and I wanted to catch hold of her and ask, 'Can I have my picture taken with you?' But you never know, do you; one day one of these stars might tell me to sling my hook and where would that leave me?

As for me, I always pose for a photograph. It's an honour.

I mean, who the hell would want a photo of me? I think
that to be rejected would be an awful thing. For example,
I've been a fan of the singer Billy Ocean forever and if I
ever saw him and I asked for a photo and he said, 'No way,
I'm on holiday,' I would be devastated. Especially after a
lifetime of adoring him. I'm not saying he would say that.
He's a sweetheart, really. But I think *if* he did, that would
finish me. So I always stop and talk to people and, trust me,
sometimes that's hard as I often get six people talking to me
at once. I really do try my best. Keep smiling, Chris *bach*.

CHAPTER NINE

Life with Gabe

More than just friends

WHAT CAN I SAY that I haven't already said everywhere: on the air, in books and in my shows? I am a lucky boy to have Gabe. We are getting on better now than ever and it's been pretty good along the way anyway. Gabe comes to some of my bookings and works the sound system and the backing tracks for me. He knows everything about my performing and it's so nice to have that rock there. He looks after me when I'm ill and every day tells me that I'm number one. He's good with Sam, and Sam loves Gabe very much. I worry about Gabe sometimes, as he's having a lot of trouble with his knee, and he works so bloody hard. I always try and make sure that I help as much as I can, even if it's only pressing him a few shirts, and making sure I cook a nice bit of dinner every tea time. We are both fond of cooked dinners, so every day I cook for the both of us.

I don't think for one minute that I would be able to perform as I do if it wasn't for Gabe behind me. And, of course, it's nice to have someone to be proud of me, and my God he is so proud of me in everything I do. He tells me every day. Our favourite place to be is down the caravan in Trecco Bay, and we love to go off in the motorhome together. But I honestly mean it: I don't think I would be alive if it wasn't for Gabe.

I'm trying to coax Gabe to try for a show on the wireless

as I know the Garden members love him dearly. I think he should try and do a programme about films, movies and theatre as he's so good at all that. He has a real passion. But Gabe seems happy to just be in the background, supporting me. One day perhaps I'll see him broadcasting again. He'd be so good at it. Not as if it would be his first time. He used to have his own show on Touch Radio in the nights. He had quite a following and they still phone him up at the BBC when he's answering the phones for me. I have to tell him sometimes, 'Hey, I'm the star here!' But he always takes it on the chin. I'm glad that Gabe still gets a few fans calling him.

I hope we have a few more years in us yet. I wouldn't know what to do without him.

Making new friends

During my first year in Porthcawl, new people came to live next door to me. When I say next door, I mean a football pitch away. We had a detached house each with lots of ground. In fact, I had to have a sit-down mower. The lady and gentleman were going to put their rubbish out, and I shouted over the hedge that the bin men were coming tomorrow and not today, because we always had a lot of trouble with animals ripping the bags open. We then got chatting and I found out that the husband, Paul, was from Cwmafan (of all places), and she, Pamela, was from Yorkshire. What a combination. We immediately hit it off and became best friends, which we still very much are.

Pam was the lady and saviour who brought me a huge beef dinner when I was laid up after an operation. It was the biggest dinner I've ever seen in my life. The size of a manhole cover, almost. Enough for three meals – and you know how much I can shovel in, in one sitting! Me and Pam are looking forward to taking a weekend break in Spain, nosing about, shopping, etc. And with my Spanish I'll make sure she doesn't say the wrong things in the wrong places. She's a girl, that one! When she and Paul finally decided to get hitched, I helped arrange the wedding, and dabbled with the music too. As she stepped into the chapel, the chorus blared out – performed by Il Divo just as she wanted – perfectly timed and perfectly edited, courtesy of perfect little me. Okay, we had to time the walk from the car, into the chapel and down the aisle. Under that smile and veil I am sure I could see her counting the beats under her breath. Like me, Pam likes everything to be spot on.

Pam and I are still the best of friends and always will be. Sometimes you can just tell, can't you?

Staying in the caravan

I really love my caravan. I think it's because I could up sticks and plonk it down anywhere if I ever got fed up. Sometimes I don't ever want to live in a house ever again! I can't help it. I think this gene comes from my mother, Gypsy Margaret Rose. The big thing is not having to put up with neighbours (even though ours at the moment are the best ever). The caravans are all detached and we have our own gardens. Gabe has done well with the planting of flowers, despite the weather. Even in mid-summer in Wales, it's freezing and the central heating is on, and the trees are almost horizontal with the wind and the rain. As I always say, three months of winter and nine months of bad weather…

I often hear quiet little knocks on my caravan door and then when I open it there's usually a lady with a piece of paper wanting a dedication, or dropping in samples of homemade pasties and diabetic-friendly scones for me to try. When I lived in Cwmafan, people used to just walk in and shout, 'Yoohoo!' Once, someone left a dedication in the kitchen when I was in the toilet. I have to admit I don't like the 'just walking in' business. I do like my privacy.

But back to the caravan. There's something about a caravan that pleases me. I have to admit I could live in the van and never miss a house. And our motorhome is one of the best things ever. Expensive but, hey, so what? I work my guts out, so there has to be a reason for working so hard. We've been all over Europe and it was so exciting. I just didn't know where we'd be sleeping that night. Would it be Germany or Luxembourg? Wow, that is so me. Just as long as I've got British tea bags and not the British weather. I leave Gabe to the driving.

A life on wheels

I went to see Gillian Elisa one day and she showed me her new motorhome. This is how I came to buy one. I immediately fell in love with the wagon and wanted one myself. So off I went to Barry and viewed one. I just couldn't resist it. I had to have one and so I bought a brand-new motorhome. My God, I loved it and Gabe and myself went on jaunts everywhere we could. I was great for gigging as it was my dressing room and if we went out in the sticks somewhere, we stayed the night in it and I loved the freedom.

I upgraded to a larger one with separate bedrooms instead of a put-you-up (or was it a pull-you-out?). Anyway, the places we went! One time we drove to Dover and decided to go somewhere while on the boat. As we drove off the boat, Gabe's cousin Rita phoned us and asked us to go to her house in San Jean de Luz in the Basque region, in the South of France. Isn't it nice to have relations in the South of France. I've only got relatives down by the naval club in Aberafan!

We drove down in two days and when we got there we visited San Sebastian in Spain, which is twinned with Porthcawl of all places! There was a sign there, in amongst the Rolls Royces and film stars on Harley Davidsons, saying, 'This is San Sebastian – twinned with Porthcawl.' I somehow think not, but the bay does look a bit similar. We have also been to Belgium, Holland and Luxembourg. Oh, and along the west of Germany too. I love my motorhome so much I just couldn't be without it now.

When I upgraded the motorhome, Gabe made me take it back as the curtains weren't finished properly and the weave on the seating was damaged. I suppose his heart's in the right place. He wanted an extra armrest, too, as he does most of the driving. When we go on an adventure it's like the Cliff film, *Summer Holiday*, and I'm Una Stubbs! I would advise everyone to get a motorhome. For me it was life changing. We still haven't had a bike rack attached to the back, but I've had a digital telly installed. Well, I can't see Gabe wanting to cycle in the evening after he's been driving all day.

The French/Basques are lovely and it was good to see Gabe's cousin Andoni again, and his wife Julie and their new baby Tiago (as in Santiago). We had a wonderful time. Andoni's parents, Rita and Domeka, were so welcoming and couldn't do enough for us.

We parked the motorhome in a campsite in San Jean de Luz, and Gabe's family took us around everywhere, France and Spain, shopping and eating and visiting friends. The toilets on the campsite turned out to be a hole in the floor which I missed on a regular basis. So I used my own loo in the van. On the way back, which again took us two days, we saw fields and fields of sunflowers, as far as the horizon, and I posed in the middle of them. You know what they say, amongst every bunch of flowers there's always a prick!

We often take Gabe's mam, Peggy, out in the motorhome and go to places like Chepstow races and markets. Any opportunity and she is up for going on a picnic. We also went one year to the police open day in Cwmbran and used the motorhome as a selling stall.

CHAPTER TEN

Health and Diet

It'll have to be good to catch me

MY HEALTH SEEMS TO be on a downward spiral at the
moment (January 2009). What a disaster! I hadn't felt right
since the Variety Club Awards the previous October after
which I'd had a bad chest infection. My voice was quite
affected and this always grieves me. The baby was unwell.
Bruce was, too. Then I started to get really ill and after I
collapsed I realised that I had the bad flu strain norovirus.
I became so ill I was off work for three-and-a-half weeks.
Doctors were around me daily, paramedics were at my door,
Gabe took three weeks off. Then I had to go into hospital.
When I came out I had a relapse. I was crying and asking
for my mother and in fact I could see her talking to me one
day. I was told that I came close to snuffing it... pity in some
ways, I could have come back and haunted my family. One
day!

I now look back and realise that I nearly did die. Teddi
Munro came to see me and she cried, as did my lovely
Kathryn. Countess Christine was asked to look after me
while Gabe went out to get some groceries and she spent
the whole time just rubbing my back as if I was a baby. I
couldn't walk, and Gabe had to hold me up and guide me
to the toilet. He'd put me on the toilet and say, 'There you
are. You can go now.' I remember saying back to him, 'Go
where?'

I was so ill, too weak to even wash myself. Gabe's brother-in-law Gene, the happy Cockney, was a lifesaver to me. He called every day and brought provisions for me. Lenny Dee the comedian called to see me whenever he could. Remember, I was contagious and they still came to my aid. Lenny saw to all of my VAT as, of course, life goes on.

I'm looking at this 'swine flu' thingy that's about and they say it's mild. Did I have swine flu then or was it norovirus? Who really knows? I seem to be having colds and bad chests on a regular basis but I put that down to this unforgivable weather. Welsh people make me laugh sometimes. We have months of rain and then you get one afternoon of sunshine and we (not me) say, 'Turned out nice, hasn't it?' or 'Oh, it's not so bad after all.' Catherine Tate's words as Nan comes to mind once more.

I put a multivitamin in with my medication so that I don't forget to take it as I usually do. But I have to be honest, a month in the sun would cure me of a few things and put me right in my mind. I think seeing dark clouds every day is enough to put anyone off. As I write I'm finding it very depressing here in this extremely wet summer, especially after coming back from abroad where the temperature hovers around 42 degrees. The rain is lashing down and my central heating is never off. I think to live in Wales you have to be as strong as an ox. I seem to be getting cold after cold after cold. I just wish it would stop raining.

Peter Pancreas

'Diabetes, my arse. Take a sweetener and you'll be okay.' Yeah, yeah. But that's what I was led to believe before I developed the condition. These days I suffer greatly with my legs and the pain is so bad that I sometimes cannot walk at all. I've bought a wooden contraption; it's like a frame with beads on it. There are notches on the beads and they roll back and forth and you push your feet against it and it does help somewhat. I bought it in Spain (where else?) and I've got lots of roller things and creams and lotions. You name it, I've probably got it.

If you can avoid diabetes, for God's sake do so. It's killing me on the quiet. I urge you (again) to go and be tested for it. There are, they say, about 30,000 people walking around with diabetes and they don't know it. If you leave it, it will affect you in years to come; blindness, kidney failure, amputations, all sorts. So please go and have a test and try to keep your weight down. Diabetes is treatable, so think about it – please. It's taken my mother and it's taken Ray Gravel and it'll probably take me. But it'll have to be bloody good to catch me first.

As you know, my love for children is immense and I've had a bee in my bonnet for a long time about children and diabetes. I want to start a diabetes roadshow going around schools, maybe doing a few each week in the afternoons in my role as Ambassador of Diabetes UK/Cymru. We should teach children to eat properly, not like I ate as a child.

When I grew up, sweets, crisps, chocolates and fizzy drinks were treats and mainly bought out of our pocket money. Unfortunately, between my mother's shop and my dad's chip shop I had far too much access to the wrong foods. Regrettably today these 'treats' have become part of people's main diet and we are hearing of children as young as six years of age diagnosed as obese or, even worse, with diabetes. Children should not suffer, especially when such health problems will only get worse as they get older.

My idea is to have a mascot called Peter Pancreas and really try and get the message over to the children – even if I have to inject myself with insulin in front of them to show them what life can turn into in years to come. Hopefully they will take heed of the message and start to eat better foods. To be honest it's Sam, my godson, who has egged me on this one. I think of Sam and I only want the best for him. That little one was sent from Heaven, I'm sure!

Needs must

I also want to do a sponsored slim to raise money for diabetes. Well, I'm going to have a go anyway. I get upset when I put weight on and the insulin puts it on me something awful. Recently I had a bit of a scare; a visit to the specialist gave me a wake-up call. He told me that the way I am now might knock 15 years off my life. So now I'm on a strict diet and I'm really having a right good go at keeping healthy. Since seeing the doc, I've lost three-quarters of a stone. Onwards and upwards.

Sometimes when I speak to my dietician, I feel as if I should be eating cardboard just to please him. I'm dying for a massive piece of fudge cake or coffee cake! One day it will happen. I'm going to ask for a pancreas transplant. Why not? When your car is breaking down you trade it in for a new one, or a good second hand one at least.

I'm trying my best to cook only healthy meals as Gabe wants to shed a stone or two as well. But one thing I notice is that when I was abroad the weight fell off me. As it was dry I would walk in the heat. It's all well and good eating a good salad, but in this climate here in Wales, you need something a bit more substantial.

For breakfast I eat Cornflakes with Canderel sprinkled over the top and semi-skimmed milk, and I imagine that I am eating rice pudding or cake and custard. I have marmalade in the mornings but I buy the reduced sugar one and that seems to be okay if I only have a slither... and a microscope to see it.

I find that toast with a tomato cut up on top and some rice is nice. I'm lucky that I can make paella, after being taught out in Spain all those years ago.

I've stopped eating take-aways. I had to, because of what the specialist told me. I've made up my own diet and it seems to be working. I only use olive oil and I have a spray oil to use as little as possible. All meat is grilled as much as possible and I have gone over to fish in a big way. Yellow (smoked) haddock or cod is nice, but bloody dear! I eat a lot of grilled bacon and gammon with tomatoes and lots of mushrooms – so good for you – and fresh bread; crusty rolls are my favourite but now I only use Flora pro.active. I keep away from cheese and pastries as much as possible. But I have chips every day with my Actifry 'no fat chips' and I am losing the weight. The Actifry low-fat fryer is a lifesaver. I was told about it one night and I haven't looked back. Chips with no fat, wow! There is a Heaven! I also cook roast potatoes in my Actifry – wonderful!

I'm watching what I give Sammy when he visits as well. He likes grilled Smiley Faces and he's fish mad; loves fish fingers. I only buy him low sugar drinks and he gets a plain biscuit as I do.

CHAPTER ELEVEN

You've Got a Friend

Respect

MY CIRCLE OF FRIENDS constantly changes. This doesn't mean I lose friends, but help and support those who need it most. In return they support me and my charity work whenever they are able. Like the Garden, it doesn't mean because I haven't mentioned someone that I don't I think of them. There are simply so many, but I do respect each and every one.

Putting the world to rights over tea and chips

Sarah Barry Williams owns a website called downloadfactor.com which sells tunes, mainly by Welsh artists. They can be bought individually, which I think is brilliant. I use the website just to browse, looking for new, fresh and original Welsh tunes for the Welsh Night feature on the radio. This has become very popular with the Garden and I receive requests from all over the world. So many of the regular listeners tune in via their computers and email their requests for the last Friday in the month. Unfortunately, even with a three-hour show I have no way of playing all their choices.

I eventually met with Sarah to discuss some business. I had spoken to her quite often when my CD became available to buy online as I am not technically minded and needed a lot of help to get things right. She is very clever with the computer and has helped me no end with my website.

We also hit it off big time. I was invited to see her work when she did a show in Cardiff. She is a very talented performer in her own right, a wonderful singer and a brilliant tribute act as Madonna and Shania Twain. When I saw her as Madonna, I really thought it was Madonna. She's so like her it's almost spooky.

Sarah is such a nice lady, very genuine, and we meet up regularly. She pops over to Porthcawl for chats in the day and she knows my routine. The best time to see me is about 11am and never after 3pm as my head starts drooping and I need to have a sleep. We can talk for Wales and now put the world to rights over tea and chips.

We work together quite a bit and Sarah has become a regular member of my stage shows. In addition, we are now planning a new venture for the future and we are both very excited about it. (No, we are not getting married! Ha, ha, ha.)

When in doubt, get Lenny out

I don't rightly remember how I met Lenny Dee, the comedian. He seemed to jump out of the bread bin one day. Now I feel as if I have known him for half my life, even though it's only a little while. He runs me around when he can and prefers me to have company when I'm out and about. I think he genuinely worries about me. He is a great mediator for work in clubs and is always telling me that I would go a bomb in this place or that place. He should know, as he's worked just about everywhere.

I am always impatient and want things done immediately. I remember needing posters copied and I didn't have a clue where to go to get them done. When in doubt, get Lenny out. As sure as anything, he said, 'I'll nip you round to the printers now in a minute after I've had a cuppa.' We all need people like Lenny and it's nice that there are still some good ones about. Lenny works closely with a group called Casual Affair and they have been on the circuit for years. Once, when their regular pianist Ian Griffin was away and a late booking came in, Lenny asked me to step in, just for the one night as a keyboard player for the group. I would have loved to have done it but I was already working that night. It would have been like going back in time, like the Townsman in Swansea or the Sandman in Aberafan.

Mark and the Jenkins's's's's's

Mark Davies is an animator based at the Bristol Film Studios. He approached me with an idea to animate The Jenkins's's's's's for television. Mark heard me reciting The Jenkins's's's's's and loved them. I knew he liked them as he knew everything about them.

Mark wanted to animate them and Binda wanted to make a radio show about them. I wanted firstly to show it to the BBC, but no interest was shown, possibly because it was only on paper at that time. It took about two years to get the animation done as we had to decide what the characters would look like. Gabe likes animation and helped a lot with the development of this project. We used the actors' voices from the recording that was made and it worked well. Mandy Starr plays the lead, our Gladys, Roy Noble her long suffering and idle husband Dai and Huw Ceredig is the ol' man Idwal, upstairs. Now with these three great Welsh personalities we were off to a flying start. Mark and I worked hard to get the project completed for entry into the Swansea Bay Film Festival 2009 and we were over the moon when it won in the best animated category.

Mark was with me at the award ceremony when we were

presented with the trophy. I will never forget his face when the winner was announced and I gave him the award. It's always nice to have a pat on the back. I love working with Mark and I have a feeling that we are going to be doing a fair bit on telly. With the pilot episode in the can we are hoping to arrange for the film to be re-recorded in the Welsh language. A lot of TV companies are raving about it and I am pleased that there has been so much interest shown. It would be nice to see The Jenkins's's's's's on telly. One day!

Mark's work on The Jenkins's's's's's can be seen in the published diaries. He is also responsible for the new website www.friendlygarden.co.uk and regularly updates the comic strips with the further exploits of Gladys and Dai and their family. We are hoping it will do equally well when it is entered for the American film festivals.

It's like showing a red flag to a bull: once there's something that interests me, that's it, I'm away with the fairies. Planning and hoping and scheming. So look out, The Jenkins's's's's's will return...

It's always a pleasure and a thrill to meet the stars and each time I meet a new 'personality' I get a shiver. At the Swansea Bay Film Festival we were hobnobbing with celebrities from all over the world; actors, actresses, movies directors. Michael Sheen is one of the best actors to have come out from the UK and one of the patrons of the festival. Originally from Port Talbot, he is now very much in demand. I was surprised to see him sitting in the audience and when we won the best animation award for The Jenkins's's's's's, the opening line of my acceptance speech was, 'Well, there's two successful Port Talbot people here tonight,' and he laughed big time. His mam and dad are lovely too, Meyrick and Irene. His mam came up to me and said, 'Lovely programme, Chris,' so I thought, my God, they must be talking about *me* in the house. Perhaps Michael Sheen knows of me... wow!

Slightly Offstage

I had a call one day from London from Gill Shaw, photographer to the stars. She wanted to put me in a book of celebrities that she was compiling for charity. We met at my flat in Cardiff and she started to take photos of me. She was good and I was impressed. She wanted this particular project to reflect the whole of the country and I became her contact for Wales and still am. It's always good to catch up with her and we speak from time to time on different projects she's working on.

The book, *Slightly Offstage*, came out and I went to London to the launch in some posh hotel. While I was there I met Lesley Joseph. My friend wanted her autograph so I said, 'Watch this space,' went over to Leslie and said, 'How wonderful to see you again. I haven't seen you since I interviewed you some years back.' 'Oh, but of course,' she replied, and went on to give me her autograph for my friend. We had our photos taken 'for old time's sake'. Mind you, I'd never clapped eyes on her before! Bloody personalities pretending they know one another – whatever next?

Gabe, as usual, had wandered off and was busy holding court. He really seemed to attract people. When I caught up with him, Richard O'Brien of *The Rocky Horror Show* and *Crystal Maze* fame was holding his attention, discussing future plans!

While networking I bumped into the TV presenter Jill Dando. She came over as a really nice girl and we chatted for a while. It wasn't long afterwards that she was murdered. My God, it makes you think.

The launch featured a display of all the photos from the book; big, blown-up framed photos. They looked stunning and I was proud to be included with so many nationally known household names. I gave my portrait to

Gabe. Gill is as hardworking and as brilliant as ever... and always fundraising. Her current project is raising funds and awareness for Help for Heroes, a charity dedicated to supporting wounded British servicemen and women.

My fairy godmother

Wendy Kane and myself have been friends for years. We started life together in a group which I have to admit was really good. Then she went her way with comedy and her great voice, and I went abroad, as a good boy does. Later on in life when I was very down – I had just been diagnosed with diabetes, and my mother had just died – I found myself in Swansea doing *Children in Need* for the BBC. It was all happening and I had to go on stage in about two hours' time and I sat in a corner feeling as low as you could get. Out of the blue appeared Wendy Kane. She said, 'Come on, darling, your fairy godmother's here!' and dragged me off to Littlewoods for dinner. She cheered me up no end.

Even now she organises my shows in Benidorm and has opened another door for me. She even arranged a car to collect me at the airport. I was picked up by Mick, one of her friends. He also had another guy to pick up at the same time and we travelled into the town together. Well this fella must have been the most miserable chap I have ever seen in my life. Never spoke a word and when I spoke to him politely, he could hardly say a word. It takes all sorts. I'm just glad I wasn't on holiday with him!

I went on stage in Sandra's bar at midnight the first night. It was hard for me after all the travelling. I was knackered and I had little confidence before I went on. Wendy went on and commanded the place. She was a tower of strength to me and once again gave me so much encouragement before that first show which heralded my return to Benidorm. I initially thought the audience there were from all over. However, there were a lot of Welsh in that night and I soon felt quite the celebrity. I always find that it's hard for me working out of Wales because it's outside my territory. But as I said, there were a load of Taffs in and I was so grateful for that. The following night was a dream. I also did a show in the Queen's Hotel in old Benidorm and that went well.

Wendy's husband, Chris, is lovely and was very supportive to me. He filmed me while singing out in Sandra's. I'd like to see that and maybe put it on YouTube. I have a lot to thank Wendy and Chris for. Bless you both. Wendy's done so well for herself out in Benidorm and I am so very proud of her. It really gets to me when I speak to her on the phone. There's me here in wet Wales, in gale-force winds and floods, and she sits there in front of a fan with the heat reaching 47 degrees.

I seem to be making a comeback in Benidorm. Why? I think we all know the answer to that one. I so much long to go back to Spain to live. You'll never know how much!

Hold the front page

I have to say that, generally, the press have been kind to me and I'm eternally grateful for that. The papers have supported my charity work and have favoured me with regard to my radio programme.

In Gary Marsh in particular, I have found a very good friend. He is the editor of the *Abercynon Leader* newspaper. Following an email request, I did an interview with him and we got on like a house on fire. He is a very shrewd judge of character and honest in his reporting, which I admire. His articles are syndicated throughout newspapers in Wales. He is a great believer in charity work and has supported a number of organisations greatly. My dedicated charities have benefited as a result. I cannot thank him enough for his support.

When my CD 'You've Got A Friend' became the bestselling single in Wales, I have no doubt that his coverage in the press helped enormously to keep it top of the charts for many more weeks. In this particular incidence, Diabetes Research in Wales benefited greatly from the sales, especially as it was only available through one supermarket chain, online sales and mobile phone downloads. Radio airplay was practically non-existent as I am a BBC presenter and seen as a rival to many other radio stations. But Gary couldn't wait to tell the world.

Gary, thank you so much for making my life easier. I'm so lucky to have so many people on my side, in particular you. Cheers, Gary! My handsome boy!

My own personal Bernard Delfont

Mario Romero is an agent in London who has become a big friend. Are agents friends though, or is he just using me to finance his lifestyle abroad? Hmmmm. Only joking!

We met years ago and he gave me work in the Channel Islands and in Spain, and even in Holland. His agency then was very small, but it's now grown to be a bit of a monster. He has moved up the ladder and has right posh offices in London. When I go there I feel as if I'm going to see Bernard Delfont, the theatrical impresario. There are pictures and photos of all of the big stars over the years.

Mario now represents a number of Welsh artists and has a section of his agency dedicated to us: mnblmanagement. co.uk. Mario's two sons have become like nephews to me and every time I visit them I teach them a little bit of Welsh and they love it. They've picked it up so well I swear they are half Welsh, half Spanish!

Mario, I have to say, has held me up high for years and

he believed in me when nobody else did. I have to thank him
for that. He's got me lots of work in London, too. It's nice to
have someone believe in you.

I also appreciate his advice and his looking into my
contracts. He is always willing to spend time speaking
up for me and negotiating on my behalf for the best fees,
even when the booking isn't through him. That's a true and
trusted friend. I'm so lucky to have found him as there are
some right con merchants to be had in this business, let
me tell you. He's a very caring man and makes sure that
all of his artistes are properly looked after and that's nice,
especially these days when lots of people don't seem to care
at all.

Mario wants me to do a tour of the gay venues and to
be honest, I quite fancy doing it. I'd feel at home doing the
gay clubs. Nobody would take the mick out of me – not
that many do now – but memories die hard and that's
to be expected, I suppose. But fitting in a tour would be
difficult. It could possibly interfere with my radio work
and I wouldn't like that. Radio is paramount. Something
that I need to consider, perhaps? Well after all, I have the
motorhome, so I can always rest when travelling, and inject
my insulin in private. Gabe is going to have to book time off
work to chauffeur me, of course. Where would I be without
Gabe?

High Tide

The singer Paul Child is one of Wales' biggest talents. We
had talked about working together on and off for quite
some time but could never fit it in with our busy schedules.
Until the summer of 2009, that is, when all that changed.
He asked me to do a double-headed show and we were
immediately booked in to the High Tide in Porthcawl for
two nights.

When it came to be, the first night was terrific. That set the level for future shows together and I felt as if I personally had gone to another level in my career. Indeed Porthcawl has always been very 'me'. I love living there. I prefer it to anywhere else in Wales to be perfectly honest, and it's always been very supportive to me, too. The audience had obviously gone out to enjoy themselves that night and I look forward to returning to the venue. It's such a good feeling.

While I was in the High Tide, I met some people who used to go to the Taibach Working Men's Club in Port Talbot donkeys' years ago. They reminded me about a certain time when Billy Raymond, a great drag artiste, came to the club to do his bit. There was beach ball catching in a massive boob tube; there was the snake and the fire-eating. Billy called me on stage and pulled my trousers and pants down and set my butt alight. Not something I'd do today – well, unless the fee was right! I am freelance after all. Billy Raymond from Carlisle I will never forget! (I still have an immense fear of snakes.)

I also met up with an old friend, Ronnie Huxford, at the High Tide. He was with his wife, Janice, and she had not changed a bit. Then I happened to notice three beautiful young children with them who turned out to be their grandchildren. Grandchildren? Where had the years gone?

We sat there reminiscing over the past. I almost felt like I'd gone on a time trip, back to a time when you were allowed to enjoy yourself. It was wonderful. Ronnie is a drummer and a damn good one at that. One of the best drummers that I have ever heard in my life. He reads music like he reads English and has backed so many big names. We first worked together in the White Wheat in Maesteg back in the seventies. I'm so glad that we've caught up with each other again. You never know, I might get him to play drums at one of my concerts.

Playing for the girls

I have always loved and respected Bonnie Tyler (my angel). I loved the time, all those years ago, playing for her and just being friends with her. But one lady who sticks in my mind has to be Dot Squires. I played piano for Dot several times and we got on like a house on fire. She always told me that she thought the world of me. She very often said, 'I love my gay boys.' And, boy, did she treat me good. I learned a lot from her. Things about life, and coping, and how to treat other people. I was so saddened to see the way she ended up, without anything.

I remember speaking to Dot just before she died. She asked me to play her new CD on the radio, which I did, and loved it very much. It was her who said to me that I ought to look after people on the way up as you never know when you will need help someday, when you're on the way down. I loved talking to her and she loved talking to me. We would talk about the men in our lives. She told me that I had a good boy in Gabe and I should look after him as best I could. I felt as if she was giving me and Gabe her blessing. What a wonderful lady. Sadly missed. Love you, Dot!

Life, sometimes, can be a right scream and I get to meet a lot of famous people. Through my wonderful friend Teddi Munro I have met two very special ladies, June Brown (Dot Cotton in *EastEnders*) and Polly Perkins (who starred in the BBC's 1990s soap *Eldorado*). It was strange to be in the company of these stars and yet it was so comfortable an experience.

I remember going to visit Teddi, and June was there at the time. I was bold enough to ask her if she'd do some voice-overs for my programme and she immediately said, 'Yes, of course.' June is such a lovely lady. So down to earth. She spoke to me as if I'd known her all my life. Even now, some years later, if I get to speak to her on the phone she still remembers me. Mind you, how many times have I heard the phrase, 'Once seen, never forgotten'?

June is big friends with Polly Perkins (whose autobiography, incidentally, is incredible). Polly has a nice house in Spain, and Gabe and myself have been there several times. Always a warm welcome, and a large pool to cool off in.

Polly lives near the set of *Eldorado* and we all ventured up there and had a right good look. It was spooky as I stood outside Marcus Tandy's house. I half expected him to walk out calling for Pilar, his girlfriend. The set of *Eldorado* was generally quite run down, although a holiday-home complex has been built on the land immediately surrounding it. I've uploaded some of the photos to my website if you'd like to take a look. I met the Spanish actor Franco Rey in Marbella and he was charming. He played the doctor in the show. If you ever venture down to southern Spain, it's near a place called Coin, and up the mountain a little.

My heart turns upside down when I'm there. I want so much to live there. I miss it and I never felt that I had a home until I went to Spain. I felt free in Spain and I felt as if I had arrived home.

Shirley in Spain

Shirley Stubbs is the mother of Kim, and mother-in-law of Chris, two friends of mine from Cardiff who I've known for some years, having done business together. They moved to Spain to live (jammy buggers!) and Gabe and myself visited them and met Kim's mam Shirley. Shirley used to go to school with Gabe's mam, Peggy. With Shirley and Kim it's like roles reversed. Talk about chalk and cheese! Shirley is the wild one and the daughter Kim is the quiet one. A bit like me and my mother. Shirley emails me a couple of times a week and we send each other dirty jokes. Oh God, I love dirty jokes, especially from women. They tend to be dirtier!

Sometimes Shirley says to me that it's boiling hot out there in southern Spain and that she misses Cardiff. Hmmm, perhaps we are not as alike as I thought! I like Shirley and Tony (her better half), and Kim and Chris. Maybe one day we'll be neighbours? That will lower the prices of villas in the area.

Meeting Rhydian

First of all, what a fantastic name! I watched Rhydian on *The X Factor*, as we all did, and I instantly liked him. He seemed to be an individual, like I am, I suppose, and I was rooting for him big time. I remember getting right pee'd off when they started calling him 'The Riddler'. How dare they? I watched the final on telly and when it came down to the last two, Rhydian and Leon, I knew Leon would win it. For a start, Scotland has a larger population than Wales. I was right: Leon won it… or did he? To my mind, there was only one winner from the start and that was Rhydian. I knew that he would be the successful one, and was I right? You bet I was! The song that sticks in my mind is 'Go West'. He looked like a superstar when he performed it; and what about all those soldiers dancing behind him? There is a Heaven!

A call came one day asking me to host and sing at the Beaufort Male Choir's annual concert. I have done this lots of times, once with Jason Howard. I immediately said yes and asked in the same breath: 'Who's the guest this year?' They informed me that it was to be Rhydian and I was thrilled as I am a big fan.

The tickets flew out and the leisure centre at Ebbw Vale was going to be bursting at the seams (again). People queued for ages to see if there were any spare tickets available. There were two lines of people at the entrance and it took a while to get them all in. I arrived for a rehearsal at 5.30pm with Lady Kathryn and Countess Christine, who were clutching my CDs for their lives. Gabe was following on a little bit later with his mum Peggy and his brother Ross. I was introduced to Rhydian and his opening line was: 'Thank you, Chris, for playing my records.' He went on to tell me that his parents listened to the programme and they were chuffed that I played his songs and spoke so highly about him. He was really sweet and not at all affected by the success. I immediately liked him and he was only too pleased to have several photos taken with me. He had his own hairdresser there and I nearly asked her if she could straighten mine, but I held back.

There were a lot of people darting about. Police were on duty and security were everywhere. I thought to myself, 'All these big butch men here just for me.' I was taken to my dressing room and I settled down. I had invited Mandy Starr to see the show as she only lives up the road and was not performing on that particular night. She arrived in fine fettle as usual and took her place in the front with members of the Beaufort choir. I had planned a surprise for Mandy: I called her out of the audience to sing 'Some Enchanted Evening' with me. This is one of our favourite duets and the audience loved it. It was nice to see Mandy in the spotlight in her home town. I also sang 'The Garden Song' and one other. The comedy also went down well. As usual I started with my famous line: 'Thank you to the local council and the management here for allowing poofs in tonight.' That usually does the trick.

The night was another success story and the place was buzzing. One thing that sticks out in my mind was the ice cream. The interval was coming up and the lady was getting the ice cream trolley ready, so I dived in and bought a few of them to save Gabe from queuing. I went into the audience to give the ice cream to Gabe and his mother and brother, but I was on a different level and couldn't reach them. So

Peggy had an idea. She put her handbag on the end of her umbrella and I passed the ice cream up to them on the level above. I had a round of applause for that.

People that night thought that Ross (Gabe's brother), who is a rather snazzy dresser, was Rhydian's brother. Mind you, Ross dresses like a film star just to go out for a drink. I put them right and told them who he was.

I wish Rhydian all the best. He was lovely, and to my mind he's doing things right.

Chapter Twelve

The Rain in Spain

Perez Prado on the ferry to Ireland

I GOT TO KNOW Kitty while I was on Touch Radio in Cardiff. She would phone the programme as she worked nights in a local hospital, and we became good friends. Gabe knew her, too, because he worked on the hospital radio. Kitty had met a young man called Bill and they decided to get married. Now Kitty is from southern Ireland and her family was out there, so the wedding was to be in the Emerald Isle. Kitty asked me to give her away and Gabe was Bill's best man. And so we were to go to Ireland.

However, my father died two weeks before their wedding and I felt too upset to go, and too worried to leave my mother on her own. My mother, being my mother, told me that I had to go. I wasn't to let people down. So Gabe and I went. We drove over in my little Seat Marbella and the ferry was torture as the sea was so rough. People were throwing up, and the boat people kept playing the 'Dancing Man' Guinness advert on the monitor over and over again. The music by Perez Prado drove us to despair.

Ireland was so laid back. The motorists kept stopping and blocking the road to have a chat. Gabe was going mental! We often hear of the bride being late, but the groom too? Just as well the wedding was booked to happen between 11am and 1pm. Laid back or what! But it was a good bash.

Wheelie bins floating down the road in Palma

One August I decided to take a trip to Spain and Palma, Majorca was the destination. People were saying to me it would be too hot in August, but when we arrived, after picking up the hire car, the skies grew dark and at midday it seemed like the middle of winter back home. All of a sudden, the heavens opened and I've never seen rain like it (and I'm Welsh!). There were wheelie bins floating down the middle of the road. The new subway was flooded, our car was flooded, there was no electricity, no cash points were working, no shops open, no restaurants open. It was a nightmare.

The highlight of the week had to be when we went to see Montserrat Caballé in concert at Palma Cathedral. Defended by sandbags, the concert was still on. Queen Sofia walked in with her coat on and sat in the front, and Montserrat Caballé said, *'Hola, carino,'* (Hello, love) – like you do – and the concert began. I felt as if Senora Caballé was going to keel over with age. She seemed very frail to me, as if suffering from arthritis. Her daughter, Montserrat Marti, also a celebrated soprano, was accompanying her. I initially thought, to cover the high notes. However, we were not disappointed. It was a wonderful concert and all the proceeds were for homeless charities.

While we were there I wanted to see the Caves of Drach, the most famous tourist attraction on the island, as my mother had been there years ago. We booked and queued and eventually got into the caves, which were a bit like Dan yr Ogof caves back home in Wales. Then we went to a seated area by an underground lake and waited for this wonderful orchestra my mother had always talked about. Well, one lousy boat came out with one fiddle player and a fella on a squeeze box. Then the electricity went off and the music stopped. When the power came back on, the music seemed to slide back up as if a record had been started again. Then a fella tried to take my camera phone off me as he said I was taking photos. Me? Never! Moving on swiftly... what a waste of time! I think the credit crunch had hit them early. They had a souvenir shop there also, and I wanted to buy a wooden carved bust of Chopin, who wintered in Majorca, but all they had were a few videos of the caves and even fewer postcards. Disappointed? You could say that!

Getting back was a nightmare. We tried to check in at the airport but were told that we had been given the wrong portion of the ticket, and that we had to go to another office to retrieve the proper tickets. As time wasn't on our side we ran to the other side of the airport, and were soaking with sweat as we queued, before having to run back. I still don't know how Gabe and I didn't have heart attacks. Naturally, when we got on board the plane I was screaming my tits off and complaining. Half the plane said, 'Oh, there's Chris Needs.' I met loads of Garden members on board, and we had a right good moan all the way back. Majorca and the worst storms for twenty years, and Gabe never got to see his grandfather's birthplace.

Meat and two veg in Paris

As a special Christmas present for Gabe I took him to Disneyland Paris. We went for three days from 1-3 December. The day we arrived it was a little cloudy and then the second day we went into the park itself and the rains came down. Another storm, just like the Majorca one; maybe even worse! The winds were so high that we couldn't go on some of the rides. We bought these plastic capes and mine was blown off my back within minutes. There were people queuing for tea just to get out of the storm, and the queues were over 45 minutes long. Heaven help us if we'd wanted a pasty as well! The day was a total bloody disaster and we went back to the hotel to have dinner. I was so pee'd off that I pinched some extra rolls of bread and made the shape of a man's meat and two veg out of them. Nice picture, though, and look, I am smiling!

Another time in southern Spain, we decided to take a balloon ride and guess what? The weather again was so bad that all balloon trips were cancelled. If anyone would like a comprehensive list of my touring dates, just let me know so that you can book your holiday for another time.

CHAPTER THIRTEEN

Across the Atlantic

Sleepless in Portland

I WAS ASKED WITH 12 months' notice to perform as top of
the bill in Portland, Oregon, in the States. I was immediately
interested as I'd never been there before. I agreed to do the
concert and looked forward to stepping on American soil.
Bruce Anderson was also to perform on the show, and Gabe
was to work the sound and backing tracks. It pleased me no
end that I would have my favourite people with me.

The time came to book the flights and, as I had lost my
credit cards, Bruce had to use his to pay for the trip. The
promoter sent the money over to cover the cost. Bill Watkins
was going to drive from Washington state to Portland see
me perform. And on the way back we were to have a stop-
over of one day in New York, so we arranged to meet Mae
Foy on the steps of St Patrick's Cathedral. My word, I was
honoured that I had American fans. I thought I had really
made it.

It was a nightmare packing to go. What would I wear?
My place was like a junk shop – clothes everywhere! I also
spent a small fortune on backing tracks as well as stage
wear. But eventually I did it all.

The Garden members were cheering me on, and I was
praying and hoping that the Americans would understand
me and they would they clap. I was quite concerned, but I

was going to have a right good go and give it my best shot. We were in contact from time to time with Portland and all seemed fine. The excitement grew and I couldn't wait for the time to come. Chris Needs was going to be 'top of the bill' in the States!

We flew from Bristol. The flight was going to be cruel as we were flying economy. The first flight was seven hours but we were comfortable and well attended. On the connecting flight, however, we had hardly any legroom and I felt like a sardine. My legs were killing me but it was well worth it, I kept telling myself, for my American dream to come true.

We eventually got there and were picked up by the promoter Ceri Shaw, a Welshman living in Portland. We were taken to the Ace Hotel in Portland and Bruce was to stay at Ceri's home, which was a bit out in the sticks. The first few days were fine and Gabe, Bruce and myself wandered around the town, exploring and eating American burgers. It all seemed so good. I called Radio Wales and spoke on air and told the world of our excitement. I had a few problems from back home, issues which, I have to be honest, gave me a lot of worry, but I tried to carry on as best as I could. I suffered an asthma attack and went to the hospital but was later released with a clean bill of health.

On our first day, Gabe and myself went out looking for food as usual and discovered a food place called Subway, just like the ones in Wales. We went in and met the two ladies working there, Tina and Angela. They were so fascinated with me and my accent. They loved the jokes and told me that I would have no problem with cutting it with the American audiences. We ate there nearly every day and we were becoming friends. They wanted to start tuning in to my late show. Little did I know that all was going pear-shaped as we were sitting there eating.

We noticed that there were a few problems in Portland, one being the taking of methadone. There were a few interesting characters wandering about and I could only feel sorry for them. What a state to get into. Fashion was another thing that stood out. I saw a few wild dressers. One guy had an orange cat suit on, with pink hair and he must have been in his fifties. There's hope for me yet! I also went to a community radio station and did an interview for them and while I was there I met a bearded lady – wild, I thought. I honestly believe that you could put a banana skin on your head and that would become the latest fashion. I have never seen such a liberal, wild, kooky crowd in my life but, hey ho, who am I to talk? I discovered a lot of beggars asking for sixty cents which apparently is the price of a sandwich.

While staying in Portland I met with the mayor, Sam Adams. He asked me how I should be addressed as he knew all about me and the MBE. He asked if he should me call me 'sir'. I told him that I would prefer 'ma'am'. He laughed and we hit it off BIG TIME. He interviewed me and I gave him copies of my CDs to use as raffle prizes for his favourite charity. He wanted to know if I would be coming back to Portland. He's a lovely man and he made us feel really welcome in his town.

We went to the Crystal Ballroom to have a sound check and rehearsal, where we were greeted by Ceri and his partner Gaabi. They told me that the show had been cancelled due to lack of support. I began to feel as if it was all my fault but, as I was repeatedly told by Gabe, I wasn't to blame. The reason for the poor turn-out was due to the swine flu pandemic. Following newspaper articles that week highlighting the increased problems across the country and across the state in particular, there had been a number of ticket cancellations. Mid week, the box office took the decision to block further sales both via the website and over the telephone. But we were kept in the dark and continued to publicise the events, attending functions and giving interviews. I was devastated. You can imagine driving from Cardiff to Pontypridd to do a gig and being told that the night was cancelled, but how about flying 10,000 miles in vain? I felt like crying. Boy, did I feel a failure. We sat around for a few days absolutely knocked sideways.

On the Saturday Gabe and I wandered around Portland helplessly and I didn't know what to do. What was I going to say when I got back home to the Garden? Gabe told me to tell the truth and the Garden would understand. I felt such a fool. Bruce had his little notebook computer with him and there was wireless connection in the hotel. He went online every day and spoke to his wife, Claire, and of course the baby Sammy. I believe that this little laptop and the fact that Bruce could see his beloveds kept his sanity. The baby shouted to me on the webcam, 'Love you, Chris Needs.' It helped me a lot. You know what I'm like with Sam.

On the Saturday night, I went looking for Bill Watkins as I knew that he was driving from Washington state to hear me sing. We popped into the bar next door to the Crystal Ballroom and there he was with his wife, SunHui. He was so happy to see me, and we started to explain what had happened to the show. He was so understanding, and I gave them some keepsakes from Wales. He could see that we were all devastated and invited the three of us for a trip in his big American car. We jumped at the chance as we had seen nothing of the States, and he took us to see the area. We saw the Columbia River, the breathtaking views of the Multnomah Falls and the mountains were wonderful. I was expecting a cowboy on horse-back to overtake us at anytime. This was the Oregan Trail after all.

They took us to a Chinese restaurant for a meal, and they were really what we needed as every one of us was ready to burst into tears. Bill is a lovely man and his wife equally so, and they really lifted us. They bought me a T-shirt with Oregon on the front and a picture of the falls. They went on to buy gifts for Sammy. They were angels in disguise and boy were we grateful. They paid for our meal at the Chinese restaurant and made us feel a million dollars. They wanted to take us to their home in Washington state but we didn't have the time as we were about start packing to head home. Bill and his wife saved my sanity and restored a bit of faith in America. We parted a bit teary and promised to keep in touch after this nightmare was over.

The time was coming to start setting off and we packed and headed for the airport with Ceri's good lady, Gaabi, driving us. It was just my luck that there was a pandemic when I was to top the bill. What could I do? I had to carry on and we boarded the plane in Portland and dreaded the thought of the flight. Flying is one thing, but doing an impression of a sardine was something else. I had to prepare my head for meeting Mae who was travelling down from Vermont to meet me on the cathedral steps in New York. How could I keep my pecker up and play the right part for this lovely lady who was a massive fan? I had to try.

An Affair to Remember

The plane touched down in Newark airport, New York, at six in the morning and we went to get our big suitcases to check them in straight away for the flight home. We were told we were too early, however, and would have to drag all our luggage with us around the streets of New York. I thought, here we go again, no meeting with Mae. But I spied a lady on one of the check-in desks and she came to our rescue. She checked the whole lot in for us.

We were told to get the bus into the city and so we did. New York was buzzing at eight in the morning. I couldn't get over it. We got off the airport bus at the Port Authority terminal. My God, this place was so alive. We went into Applebee's for breakfast and loved it.

We walked for quite a while but my legs eventually

decided that we should take the open top tourist double-decker bus. We saw just about of all of New York and it was mind-blowing. One of the tour guides, an Hispanic lady, was incredible and she showed us the sights admirably. As we pulled up outside Trump Towers she said that Donald Trump was not there, as he was in Europe awaiting the birth of his new wife! This lady was a born comedian and she lifted us fantastically. She sang to me and spoke to me in Spanish.

I kept getting text messages from Mae saying that she was going to be late. She had had her own nightmare journey, with hold-ups due to essential track repairs. She was upset that she might miss us. We were to meet at the cathedral at midday but due to delays we eventually met at 2.30pm, which gave us just an hour or two. The time came and I saw Mae in the corner of my eye. Clutching a carnation as arranged, we shrieked and hugged and kissed. Like in the movie *An Affair to Remember* it was so very moving, and after the fiasco of the past week there were tears all around.

We ventured off for a bite to eat and it was all so beautiful. Meeting Mae, like meeting Bill, was like discovering a new family member. These people were great fans and it was an amazing feeling that they had come such a long way just to meet me. Mae's hubby George was also a great guy. We shared jokes and things were so lovely. Mae and George were so sympathetic to me and really did step in and comfort me. We had our meal together and the time came to depart. Again this was all so heartbreaking as these people were so genuine. They had started as fans and had now become true friends.

We left Mae and George waving as we headed towards the Port Authority bus stop in our yellow New York cab. The time was 5pm and we caught the bus back to Newark. I went through the airport security with my hand luggage and, to my despair, discovered that I'd left my two mobile phones on the bus. Gabe ran back to where the bus had dropped us off but it had gone. I was nearly in tears but good old Gabe spied the bus around the other side of the terminal. He ran like mad and caught the bus driver's attention and got my phones back. Good old Gabe!

I'd already been through security once, but because I went back out with my hand luggage I had to go through again. I thought this would be straightforward as I'd been through once already. I put my little hand luggage piece through the scanner and lo and behold the alarms went off. The security woman made me open my case and she saw that I had a can of deodorant in there. She read me the riot act and tried to make me look like a bit of a dickhead. I brought it to her attention that the same bag had been scanned only ten minutes earlier. She wasn't having it, and took the can of deodorant from me. I pointed out that she hadn't spotted this can the first time around and told her that it disturbed me greatly that she'd missed it the first time. I wanted to tell her that with her incompetence we could have been killed if that had been a bomb. Sometimes it appears they spend too much time looking important and ticking boxes instead of doing a real job. It was almost like being back home. But I thought I'd better not push it. I didn't want to get arrested, I just wanted to get home.

We waited a few hours and after a little bit of shopping we boarded the plane. It was a cruel flight which took the best part of seven hours to get back to the UK. They really put too many seats in the plane; it's all business and no pleasure. Where have I heard that before?

After the long flight we got off in Bristol and felt like dying. The reality had hit us: 10,000 miles for nothing. I called Countess Christine to tell her that we had arrived back in Bristol and she was so relieved. It was raining heavily and we were so unhappy and hurt. All that way for bugger all! I might as well have stayed in Porthcawl and washed my nets. At least that would have been for a reason. As we travelled back over the Severn Bridge I was nearly in tears. I felt a failure and I knew I had to face my audience. Gabe had developed a bad chest and was coughing. I feared for him. Was this the swine flu that had hit Portland? I didn't know what to think.

Bruce was so excited to see Sammy. They are so close that I've seen the baby shake with excitement when he sees his dad. I went back to Cardiff and washed my clothes and then went straight to my caravan, as this was the only thing that could heal me. In America all I had wanted was to be in my caravan. That is the only place I feel safe. When I'm in my caravan I'm at my happiest.

While I'd been in the States this big American guy had said to me, 'I never go to the UK. It's expensive. It's cold. It's wet. And it sucks.' I said back to him, 'Oh, you've read the brochure have you, love?' We don't need telling about our weather. We *know* what it's like, but we've got to live here! We don't have rain here as such, more like a monsoon spread over a twelve-month.

I was so upset about the show being cancelled I almost started smoking again. It was hard having people coming up to me and saying, 'How was it in America?' I just answered, 'Different.' I have to be honest, Portland has put me right off the States. And to think that during pioneer times Oregon was thought to be the land at the end of the rainbow. It will take a miracle to change my feelings. Hurt and embarrassed? Don't ask!

CHAPTER 14

In Conclusion

Wild child

POOR GABE. WHAT A life he has with me: is it good or
is it something else? I often wonder if Gabe and I would
have happened if I wasn't who I am and do what I do. We
stumbled upon each other when he phoned me one night
donkeys' years ago on the late show on Touch Radio.

I suppose our lives have been very interesting and while
I'm flying high and living life in the fast lane, Gabe is always
there trundling behind with his books, supporting me to the
ends of the earth. I did ask him once if he minded living his
life with someone who is 'known' and his answer was and
always is, 'It's not the job I'm interested in, just the person.'
I suppose life must be somewhat different living with a
person like me. Gabe is always very protective towards me.
He won't let the wind blow on me. When we are out and
people recognise me, which happens a lot, Gabe gets asked,
'Are you Gabe?' and then people seem to be more interested
in him than me. I don't mind at all. I think it's nice for
Gabe to have a slice. After all, they always say, 'Behind the
successful man there lies another one.' I wouldn't be where I
am today if it wasn't for Gabe.

Twenty years on, we are still together and giving it welly
out there on the airwaves and the stage. People are forever
asking when we are getting hitched, but I don't need a piece
of paper to tell me how I feel. If we did get married, it would

be to ensure that Gabe got everything of mine and to avoid the problems of death duty. Oh, the taxes in this country! To be honest, I think we should because of my properties alone. I don't want anybody else getting hold of any of my estate. Only Gabe and Sammy. I dare not mention death in front of Gabe. He hates it whenever I bring the subject up. Sometimes I say, 'When I pop my clogs... ' and he stops me in my tracks. 'Don't talk like that. I'm not interested, thanks,' he says.

I must get on his nerves sometimes as I'm so outspoken and flamboyant. It can't be easy living with a celebrity. I find it hard keeping up a standard because, if I'm out and someone comes up to talk to me, I have to be on my best behaviour, and that's hard for me as I am a bit of a wild child. Now this is where Gabe comes in, keeping me on the straight and narrow. It's a very difficult job indeed. Mind you, because of what I do he's travelled to loads of exciting places all over the world. Having said that, I wouldn't have done half the things I have done if I hadn't had Gabe at my side.

If I was to wed I would like a special seventies/eighties-themed disco as a reception. (Any excuse for a party!) But we'll see. Watch this space! As long as Gabe and Sam benefit after my days, that'll be alright with me. Nobody else!

The older I get

Lonely? Yes I am and I wish I wasn't. I hate the drive home after the show as it's late and people are in bed. Countess Christine sometimes talks to me on the way home, especially if I'm en route to Porthcawl or Port Talbot.

I feel sometimes as if I've missed the bus when it comes to family. With the exception of one cousin, none of my family speak to me. The need for a child will never leave me, even though I know it's never going to happen at my time of life and I wouldn't know what to do anyway. Someone sent me a sort of a joke once about how to have a baby. First of all take one female, buy her chocolates and flowers, insert here, then moan and groan and then light a fag. I get them all, don't I?

I thank the Lord every day for giving me Gabe, and Sammy, and of course I'm blessed with wonderful friends. I will come to terms with my new life – a life without my mother and father – one day, but until then I will clutch straws and hope and pray for the Lord to see me through another day. I have always been full of confidence but as I get older, something is happening to me. What exactly, I don't know. I think it's a combination of a failing body and a mind still young from the seventies... and my kind of 'young' doesn't fit in today. My confidence is waning and I wish it wasn't.

I think that I am a faithful friend and I honestly believe that due to people and family shitting on me big time, I am losing my nerve. I have tried to push local singers and, all but one or two, they've all crapped on me and ignore me. It's true what they say: the bigger the star, the nicer and easier they are to get on with, but it's the little sing-along acts that have the airs and graces and think their shit is chocolate. There are so many green monsters out there and around me it's bloody frightening. What can I do about this? Well I've found out the way to go: I bloody well ignore them, and that hurts them most. They all want to be like me and have the stardom, but you have to be an individual and be yourself, and most of these hangers-on just can't cut it. I thank the Lord for my close friends and artistes.

I keep trying to stay on top of the diabetes but sometimes I feel it is beating me, the bastard. I often think, will I be here this time next year? And do you know? I don't know, nor do I care. One thing I have always wanted is to know how and when I am going to die. I remember speaking to the performer Paul Needs and he said, 'You really want to know when you are going to die, don't you?' If I knew, I would take out about twenty loans and go around the world and treat all my friends to a fantastic time. I am getting sadder by the day, and I don't want to, but when I feel the time is right and I cut my ties, I will disappear. I'll be bingo calling in Benidorm! Bring it on, baby!

I'm finding it harder and harder to walk as the diabetes is getting worse and worse. That depresses me and I feel sorry for Gabe as he has to rub my bad leg for ages in the night. It must drive him mad. Most nights I am unable to get any rest, even taking medication. I have to wait an hour at the very least for them to kick in and then they usually keep me awake.

I miss my mother and the way I could rely on her. I wish I had had a moment of madness with a girl years ago and fathered a child; that would have been incredible. I'm worrying also about Sam, how he'll get on in full-time school, and I just can't help how I feel. Mind you, I'll be seeing him tomorrow when I drop in his comics and presents from Gabe and his mam – and tomorrow comes around several times a week!

At the ripe old age of 55 I'll still hope to have straight hair and to live a life in Spain. I'd love Gabe to sell our house in Cardiff and buy a flat in Benidorm. I would keep the flat lovely and do the clubs out there, and I wouldn't have to worry any more about compliance and being politically correct at the BBC.

I don't need to be loved, but I do need to be liked and I need to be on centre stage, otherwise I will shrivel up and die. I have to make music and tell jokes every day and offend people. My God, I'm getting so bloody good at that. I went to the Mardi Gras this year and there was this stage manager telling everyone who came near him not to swear on stage. To be honest he was getting on my pip and everybody else's. A right little do-gooder. Now, excuse me, but I talk to thousands, possibly millions, of people every day on the wireless, so I took the hump a little about this. So I was prepared for him when he said to me, 'Chris, no swearing.' I simply said, 'F***ing warm today,' and then walked on stage. He asked for that! Boy, that felt good.

Sometimes I feel as if I've outstayed my welcome here on Earth, and maybe I should have gone years ago. I still want to come back as a gay man again next time, but maybe one who'd had a fling with one of those women types and have had a couple of boys. If I pray hard enough it might happen! If I had my time over again, I would probably have been a high-class rent boy, and not played it straight with work and paying tax and VAT, etc. I could be sitting on a fortune, and why not? It's the oldest profession in the world. Who cares? Someone has to do it.

My mother always said that she'd like to have had the high life and picked up rich men and spat them out, but the husband and children got in the way. My mother died a very unhappy woman, and I fear that I might do the same. I don't want to but I fear that may be the case. I'm more frightened now, more than ever, of things like flu and infections. Do you know I'm frightened to go into hospital for fear of catching something?

People today seem to put up with things more, like the smoking ban. They say, 'Oh well, I'll have to go outside for a fag.' I bloody wouldn't. What about my rights? Why are we always being dictated to? Or sometimes I've heard people say, 'There's awful about this MRSA.' Why don't people say bring back matrons? Proper matrons, not just medical staff in a different colour outfit. What was so wrong about a cost effective and efficient health service that was run with authority? We put up with what we are told to do with very little consultation. We're told it will be better this way. No government should tell me to put up with this and that, especially when you can see things are not right at all.

I am finding it harder and harder every day to do the 'normal' things in life, for example, speaking to the bank or a company to sort something out. I honestly believe that people are becoming more daft and less caring. One person at the bank called me 'Mr Maa Bey' and I had to explain that my name was Needs and the 'Maa Bey' was my MBE! My goodness, what are we bringing up?

I am turning into a grumpy old man and I bloody love it. I hope someone comes on to me tomorrow when I go food shopping and tell me they love to listen to me. That will lift any blues that I have!

Dame Chris Needs MBE

Have I planned my funeral? I want 'Passera' by Il Divo. I want lots of drag queens there, men in leather trousers and pierced bits, etc. I want to be carried out in my coffin to the music of the Village People and the song 'Go West'. And I want 'Dame Chris Needs MBE' written on my tombstone.

I wish sometimes now that I was a bit more normal, but I know I'm crackers, and I can't change. I keep looking back at the things that bad people have done to me, and maybe I shouldn't. I don't know. I look back and wonder if there was anything I would have liked to have done when I was young. I think the things I would have loved to have done would not have been possible then. For a start it was illegal to be gay. I do wish I'd been born later, say in the late eighties. Gays today have got it made. I was looking at the policemen on duty in the Mardi Gras this summer, and I thought to myself, 'Wow, the police are here today to protect me in case some homophobic dickhead has a go at me.' Now that's a change from arresting us for being gay. I saw two policemen walking together, as they do, and I shouted over to them, 'I do love to see a happy couple.' I thought, 'Balls to this, mate. I've taken enough stick from them when I was young.' Ha, ha!

Do I lie about my age? All the time, just to suit the moment. What have I learned by this age? If you haven't won the lottery and you have to work for a living, you have to learn to eat shit. I would love to be in a position to tell whoever I wanted to piss off. If I had done more appearances and bookings for myself instead of giving it to charity, maybe I could. I'm not sorry that I've done the charity bit. I feel a glow about that, but sometimes organisers expect too much from me. I am getting on, you know, and I have to bite my tongue. It's not often that I intentionally offend someone.

What would I have done differently? I would have listened to myself more and not others. I would have pleased myself and not done things just to please others. I'm glad that I've done my 'goody' things, like my hospital visits. I've spoken to so many people that have been clutching at straws and I hope that I have been able to help in even the smallest of ways.

Growing old disgracefully

Do I try to look young for my age? No. I try to look *good* for my age. How am I going to cope when I'm in my nineties? God willing, I will still have to perform. It's like a disease.

Could I cope with being in a home, or being dependent on Gabe to feed me and clean me? Not on your bloody Nellie. I've left strict instructions for the pillow to be used over my face.

I'm having a T-shirt printed with 'Queer' on the front and 'Poofter' on the back. Do I dress like mutton dressed up as lamb? Too right I do! I wouldn't have it any other way. I love my black and bling. I want to wear ripped jeans right to the very end. Poor Gabe, I must be driving him round the twist.

I hate dying my hair. It's a bloody pain in the arse, but I have to do it otherwise I look crap. I did bleach it blond once, for charity. I thought it was the bees knees and that I would never change back. Seeing those photos now, I cringe. That *was* a mistake! I also dye my eyebrows as they are ginger. It gets better, doesn't it?

But I am still here and I'm successful at what I do. I have people who love me and I can sleep with a clear conscience. Although sometimes I do feel like lashing out and poor Gabe has to put up with my moaning and complaining. Sometimes I wish I could be a bit more like Gabe: placid, tranquil and calm.

At this age I'm still looking to start new ventures, like the diabetes school roadshow to educate the children to eat properly. I can see myself having a nightclub and sitting at the bar sipping a cocktail and just grooving to the disco music... wearing black trousers and a black shirt and a ton of jewellery, of course. I can tell you now, there's no way I'm growing old gracefully, so if you hear a riot going on somewhere in a club in years to come, it's probably me in my nineties wearing leather trousers and singing 'Simply The Best'. Gabe is threatening to write a book called *My Life With Chris Needs MBE*. Watch this space, though I want to see this masterpiece before any other bugger sees it!

Thank you and goodnight

I thank you for reading this book and I hope that maybe some parts of it have helped you or even made you laugh.

Will I end up in Spain? Oh, my beloved Spain. Or will I hide away in my mother's house and keep it as a shrine? Will I sell my mother's house and move back to Cardiff, or stay in Porthcawl? I just don't know. It must be nice to have one home, one council tax, one electric bill, one gas bill, etc. What I want more than anything is to be secure with Gabe in a nice spot somewhere with a nice drive to park my boys' toys on, and be able to visit Spain or Wales – whatever the situation happens to be. Most of all, I want contentment and to be able to play music of some sort in front of an audience.

I thank Radio Wales for putting up with this old poofter, and giving me a chance to shine. God knows, they've had hairy moments with me, but after all is said and done I don't think I could broadcast from anywhere else. Then again, now that everything is digital, I could broadcast directly from Spain. Now there's an idea. All you have to do is plug a lead into the phone line. Simple, like. So they tell me anyway, but I don't get involved in the technical bits!

Tommy Cooper died on stage. I hope that is how I go, not queuing in the bank, or in the supermarket, or caught in the rain! Bugger that! But then again I've just been told that my heart is good, like the heart of a man in his twenties. At last, something is going right for me.

CHAPTER 15

Extracts from 'Living With Chris Needs' by Gabe Cameron

THE MOOD ON THE homeward journey was much lighter as Chris and I reflected on the exhausting day trip to Aberystwyth. It was the last Saturday before Christmas and Chris had agreed a final book-signing session to coincide with a personal appearance at the National Library of Wales. The town, with its narrow streets and practically every third establishment being either a pub, bar or off licence, had such a Dickensian feel. Christmas was definitely in the air and, as usual, I still hadn't bought a present or written a card. Always one to leave things to the last minute, that's me.

It was cold and bright after the showers we had driven up in. The Saturday staff at the bookstore had no idea Chris was going to be there, even though a crowd of people had started to queue and chat as if waiting for a bus. Chris, however, had other ideas as he spied Rose Crees, one of his dedicated fans from the West and bundled her into the back of the car to watch a DVD copy of a recent show on the laptop, as he had promised her.

The signing went extremely well, as did the interview before a live audience at the Drwm, the semi-circular auditorium inside the library. Chris was as animated as

usual, revelling being on stage, and I couldn't help but
wonder whether the interviewer, Llyr, had the skill and
experience to reel him in and keep to the time available. I
needn't have worried. Michael Parkinson couldn't have done
any better!

Press coverage surrounding Chris' autobiography at that
time had focused solely on two aspects of his life: the child
abuse he suffered and his distress and virtual breakdown
after the loss of his mam. The assembled audience were
invited to put their questions to him directly. Chris being
Chris was as open as ever, and the audience were most
respectful and caused neither embarrassment nor distress.
In fact, he made the evening even more memorable by
entertaining them with a selection of jokes, songs and piano
playing in addition to recounting anecdotes from his life.

When asked if he was going to publish further books,
Chris was initially taken aback; you could momentarily see
the surprise on his face. However, before he had the chance
to respond, a powerful voice resonated from somewhere to
my left. I immediately thought, 'Oh no, not a heckler, not
now.' Especially not after opening up his life to scrutiny
for an hour and a half and being recorded for posterity in
the process. Fortunately the slight figure who boomed like
a preacher in chapel happened to be Chris' publisher, Lefi.
He assured everyone that Chris would be asked to scribe a
second volume and to expect the book within 12 months.
Chris couldn't contain his appreciation or pleasure that
someone had so much faith in him.

During the months that followed, Chris' health
deteriorated rapidly – although being the consummate
performer that he is, few realised. His mood swings and bad
temper escalated as frequently as the tears and depression,
his weight fluctuated and the pains in his legs and feet
increased. His blood sugar levels were astronomical and
he was monitored almost constantly. When the increase

in medication had little result, Chris attended a specialist appointment which we believe saved his life. It was found that the diabetes had deteriorated significantly and that he now needed to administer insulin. We were informed that had the appointment not been made, irreversible damage to his kidneys would have resulted within time. Of course the insulin had to be adjusted, but it was abundantly clear from his appearance and attitude in general that the root problem had been addressed.

In saying that, Chris had (and still has) difficulty in accepting that he will need to continue injecting until a cure, or at the very least an alternative procedure, becomes available. He hates injecting and is often in pain when administering the insulin. The circulation problems continue, so that often throughout the night and occasionally during the day I have to massage his lower limbs. You will notice that he seldom walks far without stopping and frequently sits down to ease the pain. Chairs are placed at the side of the stage when he's performing and shopping is made easier as he always uses a trolley for support.

Having lost a good five months or so due to his health problems, Chris didn't feel that he could meet the commitment of a second volume of his life in time for the November 2008 deadline. At that time a good friend of ours, Mark Davies, got back in touch. He is a most talented illustrator and animator. We had been working together for a number of years on a proposal to bring The Jenkins's's's's's to the screens, and we finally agreed the development of the characters and the style of backgrounds, etc. The Jenkins's's's's's were Chris' creation from the years when he had returned from Spain. The stories and misadventures of Wales' first family were originally syndicated weekly in a number of local papers. Chris had resurrected and extended the diaries of Gladys to reach an all-new audience on his

Radio Wales night show. The stories had become a hit all over again, no doubt entirely due to the blatant use of innuendo and, of course, Gladys' naivety which harks back to the era of postcard humour that post-war Britain grew up with.

We had been reviewing the stories and scripts for the pilot episode of the cartoon, which would be used for pitching the project to potential television companies and (financial) backers. However, we kept returning to an audio project that had been recorded and produced by another friend, Binda Singh. Binda is very much a media mogul and had also seen potential in The Jenkins's's's's's. He had previously edited Chris' scripts and had arranged a recording featuring some local personalities; among them, Mandy Starr, Roy Noble and Huw Ceredig. On reflection we agreed that this original soundtrack couldn't be bettered and would mean that the project could move forward at a much quicker pace.

The popularity of Gladys and her family was still very much in evidence with Chris' listeners, the Garden, and he set about compiling the old stories, re-editing, re-writing where appropriate and writing new pieces to link and compliment the events. As the bulk of the manuscript was already in existence, it was possible that he would now make the autumn deadline for a Christmas book release although there was still much to complete. Mark supplied his artwork to illustrate the volume and specially released a number of comic strips for inclusion that had originally been produced for the website.

The Jenkins's's's's's was as much a success as Chris' autobiography when it was released and the format has been much copied since. Chris, however, was reminded that a second volume of autobiography had been promised and it was hoped that he could produce this for the following year. I had joked with him that perhaps I should write my own volume on living with him, and Chris thought it could be amusing to have us both in the book charts competing for the Christmas number one spot. Somehow, I don't think he'd be that keen on us having joint signing sessions at bookstores!

America had always been a challenge to Chris; it was somewhere he dearly wanted to visit but he'd never found the time in his busy schedule. He was also unfocused as to where he wanted to go. New York City of course, to visit all the popular tourist attractions, and the School of Performing Arts because of his love of the TV series *Fame*. (He still doesn't accept that the series was filmed in Los Angeles, when it's based in NYC.) Then there's Dollywood, Nashville, Seattle (as in *Sleepless in...*), San Francisco... the list goes on. Up until the early 1980s I had been a frequent visitor to the USA and although I would love to return, it wasn't a passion to me as such. Chris was therefore delighted when asked to headline the Americymru West Coast Eisteddfod in Portland, Oregon in August 2009. Invitations and preparations commenced 12 months in advance. Close friend and talented Welsh tenor Bruce Anderson was asked to perform at the festival also, and I was to accompany them as their sound engineer.

My original idea was for us both to keep notes on our trip to America and to compare our entries in diary form. I thought it would have been interesting to see the same journey from two different points of view. I still do, but on reflection I feel that there would be more interest in additional tales and thoughts extracted from my journals. Perhaps one day I'll open the pages once again for you to sneak a further peek...

During the weeks leading up to the trip, I was constantly asked if I was looking forward to the trip, how excited I was, etc. To be honest, I found this very wearying. I know people were genuinely interested but I simply couldn't think that far ahead. I was busy with project work and a heavy caseload that had to be cleared or, at the very least, brought up to date for colleagues to pick up if necessary. I hate going away, even for the shortest of breaks, not knowing what I will come back to.

Chris, in the meantime, lost, or had stolen from him, a small wallet containing a number of debit and credit cards. We had searched extensively at both our Cardiff and Porthcawl properties throughout the Saturday evening and Chris spent almost four hours during the early hours of the Sunday morning cancelling the cards, making certain that none had been used and arranging replacements. But his main concern was whether or not they could be replaced in time for our journey.

Another major concern soon materialised: Chris became worried that the Americans wouldn't understand either his jokes or his accent and wondered if he should concentrate on his singing. He had been promised the use of a grand piano on stage so maybe he could accompany Bruce as well? Also, appearance is everything to Chris; what would he wear? What would he need to buy for his American performance? I couldn't but help wonder, did it really matter considering that few, if any in the USA, would have seen him perform live on stage before?

Both Chris and Bruce had made copies of their music onto MiniDisc and CD as backup in case of an emergency. Their full catalogue of music had been transferred to the MP4 player which I would be controlling through the sound desk at the venue. Two days before the journey, Chris downloaded an additional backing track for a new song he hoped to include in his routine. In doing so, he deleted his complete directory, but fortunately not Bruce's. I wish that Chris would not mess with things he knows little about. I had to spend over three hours recompiling his database; time I did not have to spare.

It is to Chris' credit, though, how much he learns.

He really has become a technical wizard and practically everyone knows of his love for gadgets and all things electronic. When personal computers became popular he had to go out and buy the best there was with every conceivable programme, even though he would never get to open 75% of them because he had no need. As soon as I came home from work, I was ushered into the office and had to immediately set up the PC. All I asked of Chris was to dispose of the boxes, which he couldn't do. One of his traits! They had to be kept in case of emergency and not just if the equipment had to be returned! I taught Chris the basics that evening before he left for work and continued every evening for next few days. Once he has a bee in his bonnet (as he puts it) and can see the possibilities, there is never anything to stop him. Okay, he only uses the programmes that he needs to use and if there is a problem I am always on hand to teach him what's required, but fortunately he always picks up very quickly what he feels he needs to learn.

The nice surprise for me was that, as usual, he didn't leave me out. After I'd set up and demonstrated the computer, I went into my own room and found identical packages awaiting me. He had bought me a computer system at the same time as his own, as a Christmas present, and I spent the next few hours installing my own setup! The very same thing happened when DVD players were first introduced. Chris wouldn't buy only one, we both had to have them – and then he sent them away to be modified so that we could play region one discs. This was very much appreciated as we tended to buy most of our movies in Gibraltar and all the new American films were released months ahead of the European region discs.

It's always difficult to buy something for someone who, if he hasn't already got it, is likely to buy it before you get the chance. It's always the same with Chris, come birthdays or Christmas. What can I get him? One year I did particularly well in purchasing and keeping secret the latest games console. If I am honest, I thought it would be a five-day wonder. How wrong I was. *Crash Bandicoot* became his favourite and I couldn't get him off it for months. If he wasn't on the phone he was playing games. He really found this helped him relax and I now have to investigate which box it has been packed into when placed in storage. I am sure it's time Chris spent some time on it, especially with his 50-inch-screen television. He will soon get lost in the games, virtually becoming part of them! And hopefully he will relax enough to start enjoying and appreciating life in general once again.

Another year I bought him a digital text display for the rear window of his car. You know the type; like the messages you see flashed up while waiting in the queue at the post office or at some bus stops, updating you with their service. Now imagine that in the rear window of the car in front; bright red neon messages! There were a number of set phrases that he could switch on or off at a flick of the handset, but I was always fearful of what he might add and flick on when, say, someone drove too close. You get the idea! I think you know well enough not to annoy our Chris!

Chris loves parties, birthday parties in particular – especially his own! But there is no way you can throw him a surprise party, that would never do! Chris has to arrange everything himself; he has to have complete choice on music, entertainment, food, venue, etc, etc. There isn't anything left for anyone else to have an input on. Well, after all, it is his party and it just has to be perfect – even down to the guest list.

I am not really a lover of parties myself, although I'm usually fine when I am there and I have a lot better time than I think I am going to have. But I can always escape; make my excuses and disappear when I have had enough. I guess in this respect we really are as different as chalk and cheese. Chris thrives on being the centre of attention while I often prefer to blend into the background, people watching. Oh, the tales I could tell! In saying that, I am always the perfect host and most attentive whenever Chris has a function.

But come Christmas, I can't help but feel that he lets me down at times. I know that he misses his mam and often reflects on the family gatherings of his youth, with him playing the piano. He is bound to feel low but it's almost as if no one else is allowed to enjoy the holiday around him. It's virtually so that no one is allowed to express their joy or discuss their plans. Chris talks over them, moaning how much he hates Christmas. Believe me, it has nothing to do with consumerism; he shops enough to cancel out any global debt. He just feels that the holiday disrupts everything.

However, I appreciate that Chris has always been a grafter. He is definitely no stranger to hard work and it is true that he has worked practically every Christmas throughout his life. You have to realise that in entertainment the post New Year period is rather more than 'fallow'. There just isn't the work available. Aren't we all broke after Christmas and waiting for that next pay day? Going out for an evening is an expense that many can't afford after Christmas. Chris is no different to any other artiste and can't afford to turn down work and take a break. He is 'freelance' and doesn't have the advantages of holiday pay or sick leave; simply put – if he doesn't work, he doesn't get paid! And you can't refuse bookings because agents will soon pass you by and future work will go to those artistes they feel they can rely on.

So when Chris says he's never had a Christmas off, although it is by choice, it is also a fact. You could count the few times he has taken Christmas Day off on the fingers on one hand – and even then, you wouldn't have missed him as he works hard to record special programmes for the radio, and occasionally for television, too. However, he feels great satisfaction from knowing the enjoyment he brings, particularly to those who are living alone. But the personal pleasure at this time of year is limited for him; there is always the additional work and never being able to enjoy the festivities fully. All functions are arranged for the evenings and night time and he is not able to partake without disruption to his radio show, which by now you understand is paramount to him.

Due to the diabetes, Chris is also restricted with the rich banquet that many of us enjoy, predominantly the range of desserts that would have untold consequences should he even try them, and has to restrict himself to fresh fruit salads and the like. We try to make it special, try to make up for his mam not being with us, but then there are so many of my own family who have also died. It really doesn't matter what time of year it is, we always remember those we were close to, be it family or friends. There's my mum cooking like a maniac as if she expects half of Cardiff to drop by unannounced, while being supervised by my brother Ross. It's hell when you come from a family of chefs. All it would take is a little interference in the kitchen and all hell would break loose. Chris is better off giving all his attention to his calls on the mobile; it never stops ringing! While I spend my time making certain my sister isn't annoying anybody or touching things she shouldn't. Idle hands and all that!

The 'Chris Needs and Friends' stage shows are always memorable events, and the excursions to the venues can be just as unforgettable, both for the performers as well as the audience. Quite often on longer journeys the artistes will travel together utilising Chris' motorhome – the journey becoming more of a charabanc trip! There's the food, the endless cups of tea and coffee, the chatter, the jokes, the camaraderie and of course the endless singing; everyone practising their routines. It's like being in an episode of *Fame*. And me, just driving, humming to myself and trying not to interfere with anyone practising.

I have driven the motorhome extensively across Europe on a number of occasions (always on the other side of the road!) without any problems. I have also driven my employer's mobile office around the country frequently – but there lie some tales for another day! Back on home turf, I was involved in an incident that has become widely known. (How come you can never have a secret when Chris is about? Ha, ha, ha!)

We were heading northward to Denbigh for a BBC event, in the motorhome of course. In the rear were Countess Christine, Mandy Starr and Rob Allen. Chris was riding shotgun. Everyone appeared to be winding down and Chris mentioned that he was going to take a nap. No sooner had he shut his eyes than I noticed a kamikaze pheasant gliding across the field, over the hedge and heading down the lane straight for us. Have you ever noticed how bulky these birds are? What on earth possessed them to think they could fly? They seem to just run and leap into the air from the tops of fences, walls and slopes… and glide! I was willing him, wanting him, waiting for him to pull up. My teeth were grinding, my fists clenched tightly on the steering wheel and I was conscious of the convoy of cars I was leading; to brake would have caused even more problems for those behind. (I could have done with that text messaging display unit in the rear at this point!) Anyway, it all seemed to happen in slow motion. The bird hit the windscreen, beak first, just like in a Road Runner cartoon. The windscreen wiper pushed him down the glass and that was last we saw of him as he disappeared over the bonnet.

The noise as he hit us was incredible. The windscreen was splintered and everyone woke with a start. Before Chris could even ask, I volunteered three phrases: 'It's not my fault!' 'I didn't do it!' and 'It wasn't me!' Chris couldn't, or perhaps wouldn't, leave the cab to inspect any damage. The bird was lifelessly hanging from the grill, suspended by one wing as if trying to climb back up. The damage meant that we would require a replacement windscreen and one wiper. Annoyed as Chris was, he now had a goal for the remainder of the journey: to contact the insurance company and arrange for the repairs on our arrival.

I'm not certain if it was the relief that no one was hurt or that the damage was relatively minimal, but when asked by our companions what had happened to the pheasant, I acted out the bird's demise as if I was on *Give Us A Clue*. Perhaps the scenario was too over the top but it sent everyone except Chris into hysterics. He was not amused! We couldn't even catch each other's eyes without bursting out in laughter, always careful that Chris was out of earshot... and the Garden will never let me forget it!

Chris is a most complex, interesting, talented and thoughtful individual. He is also a very generous person, whether it is of his time or his possessions. I love him to bits and wouldn't change him in any way and, while I like to be liked, unlike Chris, I don't *need* to be liked. I like my own company as much as I like being in the company of others. I enjoy hearing the rain and watch the storms as they drift away. I love the autumn and winter months most; the colours, the crisp, misty mornings and curling up in front of a fire reading, whereas Chris would rather be baking in the sun, struggling to breath, constantly surrounded by his phones and arranging bookings for himself and friends for various shows. If or when we settle in warmer climes, I'll be sure to take my laptop to keep in touch with everyone and continue my journals. I'll also take my easel, palette, paints and brushes which have been forgotten for far too long.

To be continued... (?)

Also available from Y Lolfa:

"An inimitable radio presenter on his life's remarkable rollercoaster ride."
Roy Noble

Chris Needs
like it is
My Autobiography

y Lolfa

£9.95

And There's More is just one of a whole range of publications from Y Lolfa. For a full list of books currently in print, send now for your free copy of our new full-colour catalogue. Or simply surf into our website

www.ylolfa.com

for secure on-line ordering.

TALYBONT CEREDIGION CYMRU SY24 5HE
e-mail ylolfa@ylolfa.com
website www.ylolfa.com
phone (01970) 832 304
fax 832 782